Grammar Step by Step

Teacher's Manual

3

Helen Kalkstein Fragiadakis
Ellen Rosenfield
Suzan Tiemroth-Zavala

with Chants by Carolyn Graham

Grammar Step by Step 3 Teacher's Manual, 1st Edition

Published by McGraw-Hill ESL/ELT, a business unit of The McGraw-Hill Companies, Inc., 1221 Avenue of the Americas, New York, NY 10020. Copyright ©2005 by the McGraw-Hill Companies, Inc. All rights reserved. Permission is granted to reproduce these materials as needed for classroom use or for use by individual students. Distribution for sale is prohibited.

1 2 3 4 5 6 7 8 9 QPD/QPD 11 10 09 08 07 06 05

ISBN: 0-07-284527-9

Editorial director: Tina B. Carver
Executive editor: Erik Gundersen
Senior developmental editor: Mari Vargo
Developmental editor: Jennifer Wilson Cooper
Editorial assistant: David Averbach
Production manager: Juanita Thompson
Cover designer: Delgado and Company, Inc.
Interior designer: Wee Design Group

www.esl-elt.mcgraw-hill.com

Table of Contents

Expansion Activities

1	Nouns	1
2	Adjectives	2
3	Verbs	3
4	Adjectives and Adverbs	4
5	Prepositions	5
6	Subjects and Verbs	6
7	*And, Or, But, So, Because*	7
8	*BE*—Present/Past/Future (with *Will*)	8
9	Present Tense with *When, Before*, and *After*	9
10	Contrast: Present and Present Continuous Tenses	10
11	Non-Action Verbs	11
12	Past Tense	12
13	*Used to*	13
14	Future Tense with *Be going to* and *Will*	14
15	Future Tense with *Will/Won't* in Different Situations	15
16	Future Tense with Time and *If* Clauses	16
17	Present and Present Continuous Tenses to Show Future Meaning	17
18	Yes-No Questions in the Past, Present, and Future Tenses	18
19	*Wh* Question Review	19
20	Contrast: *Do* as Main Verb and *Do* as Helping Verb	20
21	Questions with *Who*	21
22	Questions with *How, How far, How often, How long does it take*	22
23	Negative Yes-No and *Why* Questions	23
24	Negatives across Tenses	24

25	Possessive Adjectives, Possessive Pronouns, Possessive Nouns, *Whose*	25
26	Objects and Object Pronouns	26
27	Reflexive Pronouns	27
28	Indefinite Pronouns	28
29	Count and Non-Count Nouns	29
30	Quantity Words	30
31	*A/An* vs. *The*	31
32	Article vs. No Article	32
33	*Another, The other(s), Another one*, and *The other one(s)*	33
34	*As…as, Not as…as*	34
35	*Too* and *Enough*	35
36	Comparative Adjectives	36
37	Superlative Adjectives	37
38	Past Continuous Tense—Affirmative and Negative Statements	38
39	Past Continuous Tense—Yes-No and and *Wh* Questions	39
40	Contrast: Past vs. Past Continuous Tenses	40
41	Verbs + Gerunds	41
42	Expressions with Verbs + *-ing*	42
43	Gerund Subjects	43
44	Adjectives with *-ing* and *-ed*	44
45	Contrast: *-ing* Forms	45
46	Verbs + Infinitives and Verbs + Objects + Infinitives	46
47	Infinitives after Adjectives	47
48	Infinitives of Purpose	48
49	Verb + Infinitive or Gerund	49
50	Phrasal Verbs 1 (Separable)	50
51	Phrasal Verbs 2 (Inseparable)	51
52	Verb + Preposition Combinations	52
53	Adjective + Preposition Combinations	53

54	*Could / May / Might* (Possibility)	54
55	*Must* (Making Logical Conclusions)	55
56	*Should* (Advice) and *Have to* (Necessity)	56
57	Questions with *Should* and *Have to*	57
58	The Base Form of a Verb	58
59	Present Perfect Tense	59
60	Present Perfect Tense with *Since* and *For*	60
61	Present Perfect Tense—Yes-No Questions with *Ever*, Statements with Frequency Adverbs and Expressions	61
62	Present Perfect Tense—Statements and Questions with *Yet* and *Already*	62
63	Present Perfect Tense—Questions with *How many times* and *How long*	63
64	Contrast: Past vs. Present Perfect Tenses	64

Review Tests

Lessons 1-5	65
Lessons 6-9	67
Lessons 10-13	69
Lessons 14-17	71
Lessons 18-20	73
Lessons 21-24	75
Lessons 25-28	77
Lessons 29-33	79
Lessons 34-37	81
Lessons 38-40	83
Lessons 41-45	85
Lessons 46-49	87
Lessons 50-53	89
Lessons 54-58	91
Lessons 59-61	93
Lessons 62-64	95

Answer Keys

Student Book Answer Key	97
Expansion Activities Answer Key	157
Review Tests Answer Key	173

To The Teacher

Grammar Step by Step 3 is the third in a three-level series of beginning to high intermediate books offering extensive grammar practice for young adult and adult learners. *The Grammar Step by Step* Teacher's Manual, a valuable resource for teachers, contains reproducible Expansion Activities and Review Tests and an Answer Key for each component.

The Teacher's Manual greatly reduces teacher prep time by offering a review test for each group of Student Book lessons, for a total of 16 two-page tests. The 64 reproducible expansion activities, one for each two-page lesson in the Student Book, offer additional practice on the grammar points covered in the Student Book. Teachers and students working in an intensive instructional setting can take advantage of the wealth of expansion activities in the Teacher's Manual to supplement the Student Book materials. Alternately, teachers can assign the expansion activities for homework or extra practice to meet the individual needs of students. The Answer Keys at the back of the Teacher's Manual cover Student Book lessons, Expansion Activities, and Review Tests.

Lesson 1

Expansion Activity
Nouns

Name _____ Date _____

A Find the mistakes. Make the corrections.

Benjamin is ~~an~~ ᵃ young man. He is from mexico. Now he lives in Brasilia. His two sister live with him. He has one younger brothers in Mexico. Benjamin works in a factories in Brasilia. He has many friend. His best friend's name is joao.

B Complete the paragraph with true information about your life. Use capital letters for proper nouns. Then read your paragraph to a partner.

My name is _____. I am from _____. Now I live in _____. In this city, there are many _____. I really like the _____. I don't like the _____. On weekends, I often go to _____.

C Write a short paragraph about the life of someone you know. Underline the nouns.

_____
_____
_____
_____
_____
_____
_____
_____

LESSON 2

Expansion Activity
Adjectives

Name _____ Date _____

A Write four sentences for each topic below. Use at least one adjective per sentence. Circle the adjectives. Then read your descriptions to a partner.

1. Describe your city.

   My city, St. Petersburg, Florida, is really (big) and (crowded). The weather is (beautiful). Most days are (sunny) and (warm). There are (wonderful) beaches.

2. Describe your home.

3. Describe your best friend.

4. Describe your country.

LESSON 3

Expansion Activity
Verbs

Name _____ Date _____

A Read the paragraph below. Underline the main verbs. Circle the helping verbs.

My Life in Indiana

My name <u>is</u> Abeer. I came here from Bangladesh 12 years ago. I studied English for two years and then entered a university. I ⓓⓘⓓⓝ'ⓣ have much money, but I got a scholarship. I majored in computer science. I graduated, and now I'm working as a computer programmer. I'm not married, but I am going out with Paloma, a young woman from Mexico. We are getting married next year. We will move to Chicago because there are many programming jobs there. I miss Bangladesh, and Paloma misses Mexico, but we want to stay in the U.S.

B Write a paragraph about your life. Use the paragraph above as a model. Underline the main verbs. Circle the helping verbs.

_____
_____
_____
_____
_____
_____
_____
_____

Lesson 4

Expansion Activity
Adjectives and Adverbs

Name _____ Date _____

A Complete the table with the adverb forms of the adjectives provided.

Adjective	Adverb	Adjective	Adverb
careful	carefully	fluent	
fast		early	
clear		slow	
good		smooth	
late		hard	

B Complete the sentences below with an adjective or adverb. Several answers are possible.

1. Kim works as a receptionist in a/an _____big_____ company in Seoul, Korea.

2. She speaks Korean, Japanese, and English _____.

3. She is a _____ worker.

4. At night, she takes business classes at a university. She studies _____.

5. She is doing _____ in her classes.

6. On the weekends, she is usually too _____ to go out with her friends.

7. She tries to exercise and eat well because she knows she needs to stay _____.

8. Once a year, Kim takes a _____ vacation with her friends.

EXPANSION ACTIVITIES

LESSON 5

Expansion Activity
Prepositions

Name _____ Date _____

A Read the paragraph below. Underline the prepositions.

Pierre's Life

Pierre lives <u>in</u> Paris. He works in a large office building from 9:00 to 5:00. He drives to his office every day. In his car, he often listens to classical music on the radio. In the evening, Pierre goes home and waits for his daughter Monique to get home from school. Last summer, Pierre and Monique traveled across the United States together. They drove through some beautiful areas, including the Grand Canyon. They also drove around New York and Boston, their two favorite cities. They traveled for four weeks then returned to France.

B Write a paragraph about your life. Use the paragraph above as a model. Underline the prepositions. Then read your paragraph to a partner.

_____
_____
_____
_____
_____
_____
_____
_____

EXPANSION ACTIVITIES

Lesson 6

Expansion Activity
Subjects and Verbs

Name _____ Date _____

A Sandra is talking about her family photos. Complete the sentences with the correct subject pronoun.

1. This is my brother Tran. ___He___ lives in California with his wife Karen.

2. _____ is my sister May. She lives with my parents in Canada.

3. These are my grandparents. _____ are Canadian citizens now.

4. They live in Toronto. _____ is a beautiful city.

5. My sister and I want to see each other this year. _____ miss each other.

6. This is my brother Li. _____ lives in California, so he sees Tran a lot.

B Write a paragraph about your family. Where do they live? What do they do? Underline the subject of each sentence. Circle the verbs. Then read your paragraph to a partner.

_____
_____
_____
_____
_____
_____
_____

EXPANSION ACTIVITIES

Lesson 7

Expansion Activity
And, Or, But, So, Because

Name _____ Date _____

A Complete the sentences below using *and*, *or*, *but*, *so*, or *because*. Add commas if necessary.

1. Sandra is confused _____ she has two boyfriends.

2. She can't decide who to date. Mark is handsome _____ John is nice.

3. Sandra was angry at Mark _____ he didn't remember her birthday.

4. Last week, John called Sandra _____ bought her flowers.

5. John is nice to Sandra _____ she likes him a lot.

6. Will she go to the dance with Mark, _____ will she go with John?

B Respond to the questions and statements below. Use the word in parentheses. Then share your answers with a partner.

1. Describe two of your friends. How are they different? (but)
    Jaime is always happy, but Motoki is sometimes sad.

2. Who is your best friend? Why do you like him or her? (so)
    _____

3. Describe two people in your family. How are they different? (but)
    _____

4. What are you going to do next Saturday night? Give two possibilities. (or)
    _____

5. When were you angry at someone? Why were you angry? (because)
    _____

6. Describe someone in your family. Use two adjectives. (and)
    _____

EXPANSION ACTIVITIES

Lesson 8

Expansion Activity
BE—Present/Past/Future (with *Will*)

Name _____ Date _____

A Write five **yes-no** questions for another student in your class. Ask about his or her childhood, current life, and plans for the future. Use the verb **BE** in each sentence.

1. <u>Were you born in a big city?</u>
2. _____
3. _____
4. _____
5. _____
6. _____

B Find a partner. Ask him or her your questions. On a separate piece of paper, take notes during the interview. Then write a paragraph about your partner on the lines below.

_____
_____
_____
_____
_____
_____
_____

Lesson 9

Expansion Activity
Present Tense with *When*, *Before*, and *After*

Name _____ Date _____

A Look at the timeline below. Write five sentences about David's day using **when**, **before**, and **after**.

7:00	8:00	8:30	4:00	6:00	8:00	10:00
get up	take bus	get to school	school ends	eat dinner	watch TV	go to bed
take shower	to school	go to homeroom	talk to friends		do homework	

1. When David gets up, he takes a shower.
2. _____
3. _____
4. _____
5. _____
6. _____

B Now draw a timeline of your day. Write five or six events on your timeline. Then write six sentences using **when**, **before**, and **after**.

_____→

1. _____
2. _____
3. _____
4. _____
5. _____
6. _____

EXPANSION ACTIVITIES

Lesson 10

Expansion Activity
Contrast: Present and Present Continuous Tenses

Name _____ Date _____

A Find the mistakes. Rewrite the sentences.

1. I am often having problems with English.
   I often have problems with English.

2. Lynn and Janet sometimes are calling each other.
   _____

3. They once a week meet for coffee.
   _____

4. Right now, they listen to Mylo singing.
   _____

5. Are they practice tonight?
   _____

6. Always they spend New Year's Eve together.
   _____

B Complete the sentences with true information about your life. Use the present or present continuous tense. Then read your sentences to a partner.

1. On weekends, I usually _sleep late_.

2. Right now, I _____.

3. I often _____.

4. Once or twice a week, I _____.

5. Every Saturday, I _____.

6. Next week, I _____.

Lesson 11

Expansion Activity
Non-Action Verbs

Name _____ Date _____

A Read the paragraph below. Underline all of the non-action verbs.

Dear Annie,

    My name <u>is</u> Andy. I attend high school now, but I'm entering college next September. I want to study English literature because I love poetry, and I am thinking about studying poetry someday. My parents think that it's a bad idea. They want me to study engineering or business so that I will have a comfortable life. I really disagree with them. I'm having trouble talking to them. What should I do?

                              Sincerely,
                              Confused in New York

B Write a letter to *Dear Annie* about a problem that you are having. Include as many non-action verbs as possible. Some examples are: **have**, **feel**, **cost**, **like**, **hate**, **know**, **belong**, and **own**. Then read your paragraph to a partner.

Dear Annie,

_____

_____

_____

_____

_____

_____

_____

                              Sincerely,

                              _____

LESSON 12

Expansion Activity
Past Tense

Name _____ Date _____

A Write the past tense of the verbs in the blanks.

1. travel   _traveled_   8. go   _____

2. visit   _____   9. come   _____

3. buy   _____   10. catch   _____

4. want   _____   11. do   _____

5. make   _____   12. decide _____

6. miss   _____   13. fall   _____

7. have   _____   14. use   _____

B Complete the sentences using the past tense. Make true statements about yourself. Then read your sentences to a partner.

1. Last week, I _caught a cold_____.

2. Ten years ago, I _____.

3. Last month, I (not) _____.

4. Yesterday, I _____.

5. Last year, I _____.

6. Two days ago, I (not) _____.

7. Last weekend, I _____.

LESSON 13

Expansion Activity
Used to

Name _____ Date _____

A Write five questions with **used to** for another student in your class. Ask about his or her childhood. How was it different from his or her life now? What activities did he or she used to do that he or she doesn't do now?

1. <u>Did your life used to be easy when you were a child?</u>
2. _____
3. _____
4. _____
5. _____
6. _____

B Find a partner. Ask him or her your questions. Take notes during the interview on a separate piece of paper. Then write a paragraph about your partner on the lines below. Read your paragraph to the class.

<u>My partner has a very interesting past.</u>
_____
_____
_____
_____
_____
_____
_____

LESSON 14

Expansion Activity
Future Tense with *Be going to* and *Will*

Name _____ Date _____

A Find the mistakes. Rewrite the sentences. One sentence is correct.

1. Are you to going to go to the party tomorrow?
   Are you going to go to the party tomorrow?

2. No, I will be probably with Martine.

3. When is she going to leaving for Brazil?

4. She going to leave the day after tomorrow.

5. Will she to stay there a long time?

6. I think that she'll stay there for a very long time!

B Write each set of words in the correct order to make a statement or a question.

1. (to Brazil/next/Martine/is/to/go/month/going)
   Is Martine going to go to Brazil next month ?

2. (national/team/she/is/to/soccer/going/Brazil's/watch)
   _____ .

3. (think/Brazil/does/will/she/that/win)
   _____ ?

4. (probably/come/back/home/soon/she/won't)
   _____ .

Lesson 15

Expansion Activity
Future Tense with *Will/Won't* in Different Situations

Name _____ Date _____

A Use statements with **will** or **won't** to complete the dialogues.

1. Your best friend Lee is getting married in two months.
   Lee: Will you be the best man?

   You: <u>Yes, I'll be your best man.</u>

2. You have $1,000, but you need it for college tuition. Lee needs $500 for his fiancé's ring.
   Lee: Will you loan me $500?

   You: _____

3. Lee is worried about getting married. He wants to have a strong marriage.
   Lee: I'm afraid that Joanne and I will fight with each other and get a divorce.

   You: _____

4. Lee's sister Emily is planning the wedding.
   Emily: Please don't be late for the wedding rehearsal. It starts exactly at 7:00!

   You: _____

5. Emily needs someone to pick up flowers before the wedding. You want to help.
   Emily: Someone has to pick up the flowers.

   You: _____

6. Lee and Joanne are leaving for a honeymoon in Hawaii right after the wedding reception. You have a big car.
   Lee: We don't have a ride to the airport.

   You: _____

7. The wedding is tomorrow. Lee and Joanne want to take wedding pictures in the park. You know that the weatherman predicted rain for tomorrow.
   Joanne: Let's take our wedding pictures in the park.

   You: _____

8. The wedding starts in one hour. No one knows where Joanne is.
   Joanne's father: There's a terrible traffic jam on the highway.

   You: _____

EXPANSION ACTIVITIES

Lesson 16

Expansion Activity
Future Tense with Time and *If* Clauses

Name _____ Date _____

A Read the paragraph below. Underline the time and *if* clauses.

My name is Karl. I just started a computer company in Germany. <u>If business is good this year</u>, I will have to travel a lot next year. That will be hard for my family and me. If I have to spend a lot of time in other cities, I won't see my family very much. I will have to change something if I have to keep traveling. My family is too important to me! After I get more business, I'll hire an assistant. When there is a sales trip, my assistant will go instead of me. Before I make enough money to hire an assistant though, I will have to do all of the traveling. When I am traveling, I will call my family and talk to them as much as possible. That will help us all feel better. If business is good this year, I will hire the assistant next year. That will solve my problem!

B Write a paragraph about a problem that you have in your life. What are some possible solutions? Write at least four sentences that use time and *if* clauses to express future meaning

_____
_____
_____
_____
_____
_____
_____

Lesson 17

Expansion Activity
Present and Present Continuous Tenses to Show Future Meaning

Name _____ Date _____

A In the calendar below, write one activity that you will do on each day next week. Then find a partner and ask about his or her plans for next week. Use the present continuous tense in your questions and answers.

EXAMPLE: *What are you doing on Monday?*
I'm playing tennis.

Monday	Tuesday	Wednesday	Thursday	Friday	Saturday	Sunday
play tennis						

B Read the conversation. Answer the questions using the words in parentheses. Use the present tense to show future meaning.

Lim: I need a ride to the airport tomorrow.

Rick: I'll take you. What time does your flight leave?

Lim: (1. leave/noon) _____

Rick: No problem. We can leave at 10:00.

Lim: But I have to stop at the drugstore before my flight. I have to pick up a prescription.

Rick: What time does the drugstore open?

Lim: (2. open/10:00) _____

Rick: OK. So we should leave here at 9:30.

Lim: And I have to drop off my dog Jacko at the kennel. They're taking care of him.

Rick: Well, what time does the kennel open?

Lim: (3. open/9:00) _____

Rick: Maybe we should leave here at 8:30, then.

Lim: That sounds good. You know, I'm a little worried about how I'm going to get to my brother's house once I arrive.

Rick: What time does your flight arrive?

Lim: (4. arrive/midnight) _____

Rick: That's really late. When does the airport shuttle stop?

Lim: (5. stop/1:00 a.m.) _____

Rick: You can take the shuttle, then. No problem.

LESSON 18

Expansion Activity
Yes-No Questions in the Past, Present, and Future Tenses

Name _____ Date _____

A Write **yes-no** questions for the answers below.

1. <u>Was Lee born in the United Kingdom?</u>

   Yes, Lee was born in the United Kingdom.

2. _____

   No, Lee and his sister didn't grow up in Asia. They grew up in Berlin, Germany.

3. _____

   Yes, he really likes studying English.

4. _____

   No, he isn't going to stay here. He's going back to Berlin after he finishes this semester.

5. _____

   Yes, he'll be sad when the semester is over.

6. _____

   Yes, his parents are traveling in England now.

7. _____

   No, they didn't teach Chinese at Cambridge University. They taught German.

8. _____

   Yes, they were good teachers.

9. _____

   No, they don't teach now. They are retired.

10. _____

    Yes, Lee and his sister met them in Paris last year.

Lesson 19

Expansion Activity
Wh Question Review

Name _____ Date _____

A Interview a classmate about his or her experience with high school and college and about his or her future plans. Use the question word and the verb tense in parentheses.

1. What (present)
   _What classes are you taking now?_____

2. Where (past)
   _____

3. When (future)
   _____

4. Who (future)
   _____

5. Why (present)
   _____

6. How (past)
   _____

7. What (past)
   _____

8. When (future)
   _____

9. Why (future)
   _____

10. How (past)
    _____

LESSON 20

Expansion Activity
Contrast: *Do* as Main Verb and *Do* as Helping Verb

Name _____ Date _____

A Write each set of words in the correct order to make a statement or a question.

1. his/always/James/best/does
   _James always does his best_____.

2. hard/does/he/at/work/school
   _____?

3. does/he/homework/always/his
   _____.

4. doesn't/sleep/he/Saturdays/on/late
   _____.

5. in/did/high school/hard/study/he
   _____?

6. did/high school/well/he/very/in
   _____.

7. dishes/dinner/he/the/after/do/does
   _____?

8. doesn't/roommate/around the house/John's/do/anything
   _____.

9. room/yesterday/he/clean/his/didn't
   _____.

10. the/do/dishes/didn't/he
    _____.

LESSON 21

Expansion Activity
Questions with *Who*

Name _____ Date _____

A Change the underlined words to **who** and write a **Who** question for each answer.

1. Q: <u>Who is your best friend?</u>
   A: My best friend is <u>Jose</u>.

2. Q: _____
   A: I live with <u>Mr. Chung</u>.

3. Q: _____
   A: <u>I</u> talked to Cindy yesterday.

4. Q: _____
   A: Martin is going to go to the movies with <u>Andrew</u> this weekend.

5. Q: _____
   A: <u>Cathy</u> is with Martin right now.

6. Q: _____
   A: Charlene spent the weekend with <u>her sister Gail</u>.

B Write five **who** questions to ask a partner. Find out who your partner spends time with at school, work, or home. Write at least two sentences in which **who** is NOT the subject. Then ask your partner the questions.

1. <u>Who did you eat dinner with last night?</u>

2. _____

3. _____

4. _____

5. _____

6. _____

LESSON 22

Expansion Activity

Questions with *How, How far, How often, How long does it take*

Name _____ Date _____

A Read the paragraph below. Then write eight questions with **How**, **How far**, **How often**, and **How long does it take** about what you read.

John is a software engineer at a large company in Atlanta, Georgia. He works on a team developing marketing software. He really loves his job because it's very creative. John lives in the suburbs about 20 miles south of Atlanta. He drives to work with his colleague Maria. It takes about 30 minutes to get to work. Maria and John take turns driving. On Wednesdays, Maria and John both work at home. They use laptop computers to connect to their company. John has to go overseas to meet customers once or twice a year. Last year, he went to Shanghai, China and Sao Paolo, Brazil. He really liked the food in Shanghai and the people in China, and he loved the music in Brazil.

1. How does John like his job?
2. _____
3. _____
4. _____
5. _____
6. _____
7. _____
8. _____
9. _____

B Find a partner. Take turns asking each other your questions from exercise A.

Lesson 23

Expansion Activity
Negative Yes-No and *Why* Questions

Name _____ Date _____

A Write negative **yes-no** or **Why** Questions for the following situations.

1. You are with Greta, an old friend, in your apartment in Chicago. Greta wants to go out to a restaurant and then go dancing. You are surprised because she just flew in from Munich, Germany.

   Aren't you tired? Don't you want to stay home tonight?

2. Your son is a high school student. He doesn't like to do his homework. It's Monday night, and he has school the next day. He tells you that he wants to go to the restaurant with you and Greta. You ask about his homework.

   _____

3. After eating at the restaurant, Greta has a bad headache. You think that she should take an aspirin.

   _____

4. You and Greta have a friend named Todd. Six months ago, Todd told you and Greta that he was moving to New York City. Greta says that she saw Todd near your apartment. You are very surprised. You ask her about it.

   _____

5. You and Greta see your sister Brenda in the restaurant. It's Monday night, and she usually works very late on Mondays. You are surprised and ask her about it.

   _____

B Greta is telling you about a problem she is having with her boyfriend. Write a short dialogue between you and Greta. Write at least two negative questions and two suggestions with **why**.

_____

_____

_____

_____

_____

EXPANSION ACTIVITIES

LESSON 24

Expansion Activity
Negatives across Tenses

Name _____ Date _____

A Complete the sentences with the words below. More than one answer is possible.

isn't   doesn't   didn't   can't   aren't   couldn't   shouldn't   won't

1. Katrina __isn't__ a very good swimmer. She can't hold her breath under water.

2. Katrina _____ go to the pool yesterday because it was closed.

3. She _____ swim right after she eats lunch.

4. She could dive very well when she was five years old, but now she _____ dive well.

5. She knew all of the different swimming strokes at one time, but now she _____ know them all.

6. She wanted to go to Hawaii for Christmas, but she _____ go because she was sick.

7. Her friends are having a party tonight, but she _____ be there because she's still feeling bad.

8. Katrina's parents wanted to go to a movie, but they _____ going to go because they're worried about Katrina.

B Write five negative sentences about an activity. Use a variety of negatives such as **isn't**, **aren't**, **weren't**, **didn't**, **shouldn't**, **couldn't**, and **won't**. Then read your sentences to a partner.

1. _I can't swim very well._
2. _____
3. _____
4. _____
5. _____
6. _____

24   EXPANSION ACTIVITIES

LESSON 25

Expansion Activity

Possessive Adjectives, Possessive Pronouns, Possessive Nouns, *Whose*

Name _____ Date _____

A Kim and Lee are talking about their apartment. Complete the sentences with the correct possessive form of the words in parentheses.

Kim: I really like 1. (we) __our__ apartment.

Lee: I do too. 2. (It) _____ ceilings are really high, and it has great views.

Kim: And 3. (you) _____ bedroom is great! I like it better than 4. (my) _____.

Lee: It's too bad that 5. (we) _____ living room is so small.

Kim: Yeah, and I don't like 6. (it) _____ carpet.

Lee: June and Viggo have a great apartment! 7. (They) _____ living room is really big.

Kim: Yeah. It's much bigger than 8. (we) _____.

Lee: But at least 9. (we) _____ view is better than 10. (they) _____.

B Find a partner. Look around your classroom. With your partner, write five questions with **whose**. Then write two answers to your questions, one with a name and one with a pronoun.

1. _Whose purse is that? It's Maria's purse. It's her purse._

2. _____

3. _____

4. _____

5. _____

6. _____

LESSON 26

Expansion Activity
Objects and Object Pronouns

Name _____ Date _____

A Complete the sentences with the correct object pronoun for the word or words in parentheses.

1. I saw (Diana) __*her*__ last night at the jewelry store.

2. She liked (a diamond necklace) _____ very much.

3. When she put it on, she said to (I) _____, "It's very beautiful!"

4. After a while, she bought (two necklaces) _____.

5. They looked very good on (she) _____.

6. After she bought the necklaces, she showed them to (her husband) _____.

B Write a short paragraph about something that you bought recently. Use at least five object pronouns and five object nouns. Circle the object pronouns and underline the object nouns. Then read your paragraph to a partner.

_____
_____
_____
_____
_____
_____
_____
_____

Lesson 27

Expansion Activity
Reflexive Pronouns

Name _____ Date _____

A Write true answers to the following questions. Answer in complete sentences.

1. When did a friend of yours hurt himself or herself?
   My friend Gabriel hurt himself in a car accident last week.

2. Where can you make yourself at home?
   _____

3. When was the last time that you bought something for yourself?
   _____

4. Where do you enjoy yourself?
   _____

5. Do you and your best friend behave yourselves at parties?
   _____

6. Do you take care of yourself? Give an example of something that you do.
   _____

7. Do you live by yourself?
   _____

8. When your friends or relatives visit you, do they help themselves to food and drinks?
   _____

9. Who in your family never gives himself or herself a break?
   _____

10. When you get a headache, does it go away by itself, or do you take aspirin?
    _____

Lesson 28

Expansion Activity
Indefinite Pronouns

Name _____ Date _____

A Find the mistakes. Rewrite the sentences.

1. I don't know something about the people in my class.
   <u>I don't know anything about the people in my class.</u>

2. Everybody else are always having fun.
   _____

3. I don't have some money to travel during vacations.
   _____

4. I'm not going to go somewhere for New Year's Eve.
   _____

5. I'm not doing nothing interesting.
   _____

6. Next year, I'm going to do anything to change my life!
   _____

7. Sometimes I feel that no one don't like me.
   _____

B Complete the sentences by expressing your feelings about your life and the people that you know. Then read your sentences to a partner.

1. Everybody <u>in this class is really friendly.</u>

2. No one _____

3. Anybody _____

4. Everybody _____

5. Everything _____

6. Nothing _____

7. Someone should _____

8. Nobody should _____

EXPANSION ACTIVITIES

Lesson 29

Expansion Activity
Count and Non-Count Nouns

Name _____ Date _____

A Look at the list of nouns below. Write each noun in the correct box.

apartment	belt	boot	butter	coffee	equipment
flashlight	fun	furniture	homework	information	jewelry
knife	music	sand	shoe	sleeping bag	sugar
tent	water	weather			

Count Nouns

Non-Count Nouns

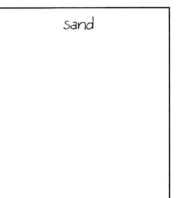

sand

B Find a partner. Imagine you are going camping together. You are talking about the supplies you need. One student asks about the supplies and the other student says whether you have them or need to get them. Follow the model below.

EXAMPLE:

Student 1: *We need a flashlight.*

Student 2: *OK. That's no problem. We have two flashlights.*

Student 1: *We also need coffee.*

Student 2: *We're out of coffee. We'll have to go to the store.*

Student 1: *We need a tent.*

Student 2: *No problem. We have a tent.*

Student 1: *And we need toothpaste.*

Student 2: *We don't have toothpaste.*

EXPANSION ACTIVITIES **29**

LESSON 30

Expansion Activity
Quantity Words

Name _____ Date _____

A Read the paragraph. Then use the quantity words in parentheses to write nine sentences about Shanghai.

    Shanghai, China is an exciting city with both good and bad qualities. Because it is a business center for China, Shanghai is an extremely busy place. Hundreds of large international corporations have offices there, and millions of people live there. So it is very crowded. During the day, the traffic moves very slowly, and the streets are noisy. The pollution in Shanghai is sometimes terrible. The large number of cars is part of the problem, but smoke is an even bigger problem. On cool nights, people burn wood in their stoves, and smoke fills the night air. On the good side, Shanghai has wonderful restaurants. There are Chinese, Japanese, French, Thai, and Russian restaurants throughout the city. Shanghai also has beautiful architecture. Some neighborhoods are full of magnificent old buildings, and in the downtown area, modern skyscrapers go up continuously. Shanghai is a special place that you really need to visit to understand.

1. (so many) _There are so many restaurants in Shanghai._

2. (a lot of) _____

3. (some) _____

4. (so much) _____

5. (so many) _____

6. (too much) _____

7. (too many) _____

8. (any) _____

9. (much) _____

10. (many) _____

LESSON 31

Expansion Activity
A/An vs. The

Name _____ Date _____

A Complete the conversation with **a**, **an**, or **the**.

Juan: What's your neighborhood like?

Ali: Well, it's really nice. It's on the side of (1.) __a__ big hill.

Juan: Can you see much from your house?

Ali: Yes, there is (2.) _____ excellent view.

Juan: What can you see?

Ali: You can see (3.) _____ big lake and (4.) _____ beautiful forest. (5.) _____ lake usually has sailboats on it.

Juan: What's in the neighborhood?

Ali: Well, there are mostly just houses. But there is (6.) _____ office building and (7.) _____ shopping center, as well. (8.) _____ shopping center has two good restaurants.

Juan: Where do you work?

Ali: I work in (9.) _____ office building.

Juan: What else is there in your neighborhood?

Ali: Well, there's (10.) _____ large park with many trees.

Juan: Your neighborhood sounds wonderful!

B Write a paragraph about your neighborhood. Circle each **a**, **an**, and **the**.

_____
_____
_____
_____

EXPANSION ACTIVITIES

LESSON 32

Expansion Activity
Article vs. No Article

Name _____ Date _____

A Complete the paragraph below with **a**, **an**, **the**, or **Ø**.

My name is Brian. I live in Topeka, Kansas, but I'm traveling around Europe now. It's difficult moving around so much, but I have all of my clothes in __a__ big backpack. That really helps. I'm amazed by the sights, the food, and the people of Europe. I generally love _____ monuments and _____ museums, and there are a lot of them in Europe. _____ museums in Paris are the best. The Louvre is incredible. I always look for _____ good food and _____ food is great here. I love _____ pasta, especially _____ pasta in Italy. The variety of sauces is amazing! Everywhere I go, I always try to meet _____ people. Today, I met _____ very nice Italian man who was interested in Kansas. Europeans often meet people from New York and Los Angeles, but never from Kansas. _____ life in Europe is very stimulating. I may move here some day.

B Write a similar paragraph about somewhere you've visited. Write **G** over the general nouns and **S** over the specific nouns. Then read your paragraph to a partner.

_____
_____
_____
_____
_____
_____
_____
_____

32   EXPANSION ACTIVITIES

Lesson 33

Expansion Activity
Another, The other(s), Another one and The other one(s)

Name _____ Date _____

A Underline the correct word or phrase in parentheses.

1. Frank and his brother Bob are always fighting over things. There were three pieces of apple pie. Bob ate two of them. Frank ate (the other ones/<u>the other one</u>).

2. Bob had four small pieces of chocolate. He gave two pieces to Frank. Frank wanted (another one/the other).

3. Frank and Bob's mother baked two cakes, a big one and a small one. She gave them the small cake. They were unhappy because they wanted (other/the other one).

4. Frank and Bob are in a skateboard club with Jorge, Steven, and Mary. Jorge called Frank and Bob and asked them to go skateboarding. Frank said, "OK, but let's call (the other/the others)."

5. Frank and Bob went to a movie on Saturday afternoon. When it was over, Bob said, "Let's go see (another one/the other one)."

6. After the second movie, Frank said, "I really liked that movie." Bob said, "I didn't like it. I liked (another one/the other one)."

7. Frank and Bob visited their aunt and uncle in Georgia. Their aunt and uncle have eight children. Six are boys; (the other/the others) are girls.

8. After they went to Georgia, the boys visited (another/another one) aunt in Florida.

9. Their aunt in Florida has two sons. Frank and Bob didn't like one, but they really had fun with (the other/another).

10. When they got back home, they told Jorge, Steven, and Mary about their travels. Jorge was really interested in their stories, but (the other one/the others) were bored.

11. Steven and Mary wanted to go to the park, but Jorge said, "I want to hear (another/the other) story about Georgia."

EXPANSION ACTIVITIES 33

LESSON 34

Expansion Activity
As...as, Not as...as

Name _____ Date _____

A Read the sentences. Write a new sentence using **as....as** or **not as....as**. When two things are slightly less than equal, use **nearly** or **almost**.

1. My sedan is small. My minivan is large.
   My sedan is not as large as my minivan.

2. My daughter is very tall. My son is not tall.
   _____

3. Our dog weighs 30 pounds. Our neighbors' dog weighs 31 pounds.
   _____

4. Our rent is high. It's $1,200 a month. My sister's rent is $1,200 a month.
   _____

5. I used to be unhappy a lot. Now, I'm often happy.
   _____

6. I am 40 years old. My wife is 41 years old.
   _____

B Write a paragraph. Compare something that you own now to something that you used to own. Us **as...as** with adverbs, adjectives, **many**, and **much**. In at least one sentence, use **nearly** or **almost** with **as...as**.

_____
_____
_____
_____
_____
_____
_____

EXPANSION ACTIVITIES

Lesson 35

Expansion Activity
Too and Enough

Name _____ Date _____

A Read the sentences and underline the correct phrase in parentheses. Find a partner and compare your answers.

1. This is a nice party, but the music is (<u>too loud</u>/loud enough). I can't hear what anyone is saying.

2. There are a lot of people here. It's a good thing that Melinda's house is (big enough/too big).

3. I have to leave in a little while. I hope I have (enough time/too much time) to talk to my friends.

4. I just ate some pastries that were delicious. The food at this party is (very good/too good).

5. More people are still coming in to the party. It's getting (crowded enough/too crowded) here.

6. I just talked to Todd. He's (too nice/very nice).

7. I'll have to take a bus home. It's (far enough/too far) to walk.

8. Buses aren't fast, but they're (reliable enough/too reliable) to get me home safely.

9. I would ask Andre for a ride, but he drives (fast enough/too fast)!

10. Taxis are convenient, but they're (expensive enough/too expensive).

11. I don't have (enough money/too much money) for a taxi.

EXPANSION ACTIVITIES   35

Lesson 36

Expansion Activity
Comparative Adjectives

Name _____ Date _____

A Write the comparative form of the adjective in the blank.

bad _worse_____   big _____   busy _____

expensive _____   far _____   fast _____

good _____   modern _____   new _____

pretty _____   sad _____   strong _____

B Alvin has lived in Miami, Florida and New York City. He is comparing the two places. Change the bolded words into comparative adjectives, and write a sentence using the words in parentheses. Don't change the order of the words.

1. (weather/**good**/Florida/New York City)
   The weather is better in Florida than in New York City.

2. (Florida/**warm**/New York/and/have/**beautiful** beaches)
   _____

3. (Housing/Florida/**cheap**/in New York)
   _____

4. (Apartments/New York/**difficult** to find and **expensive**/in Miami)
   _____

5. (Miami/[**not**] **crowded**/New York)
   _____

6. (museums/New York/**interesting**/in Miami)
   _____

LESSON 37

Expansion Activity
Superlative Adjectives

Name _____ Date _____

A Write the superlative form of the adjective in the blank. Remember to add the word, **the**.

bad _the worst_   big _____   busy _____

expensive _____   far _____   fast _____

good _____   late _____   less _____

new _____   sad _____   small _____

B Join a group of three students. With your group, write ten sentences for a guidebook to your city. Use superlatives in five sentences describing positive things about your city and five sentences describing negative things about your city.

Positive things about our city:

1. _Our riverfront park is the most beautiful park in the state._
2. _____
3. _____
4. _____
5. _____
6. _____

Negative things about our city:

1. _Our city has the least interesting nightlife in this area._
2. _____
3. _____
4. _____
5. _____
6. _____

LESSON 38

Expansion Activity
Past Continuous Tense—Affirmative and Negative Statements

Name _____ Date _____

A Read the conversation below. Write each set of words in parentheses to make a sentence. Put the bolded verbs in the past continuous tense.

Ruth: Bret, the beach party last night was great! Where were you?

Bret: (1. I/**visit**/my brother) _I was visiting my brother_.

Ruth: You were at Brad's house? I thought that he was in Italy.

Bret: (2. Yes/he/**study**/cooking/in Italy) _____
_____. He got back last week.

Ruth: Is he a good cook now?

Bret: He's excellent! (3. Last night/I/**watch**/while/he/**cook**/spinach pie and pasta) _____.

It was incredible. So the beach party was great?

Ruth: Yes. It was fantastic! The weather was perfect. (4. The waves/**crash**/on the beach/and/a gentle/breeze/**blow**) _____
_____.

(5. A lot of/people/**dance**) _____.

(6. Other people/**talk**/and/**eat**/Mexican food) _____
_____.

Bret: What kind of music were they dancing to?

Ruth: (7. A live band/**play**/salsa) _____.

Bret: Sounds great!

Ruth: (8. Motoki/and/Juana/**walk**/along the beach/together/all evening) _____.

Bret: Really? Now that is news!

38 EXPANSION ACTIVITIES

Lesson 39

Expansion Activity
Past Continuous Tense—Yes-No and *Wh* Questions

Name _____ Date _____

A Read the following paragraph. Then write questions about Hoon's day. Use the past continuous tense and the words in parentheses in your questions.

    Yesterday, Hoon was very busy. He got up at 7:00. From 7:00 to 8:00 he ate breakfast and got ready to go to school. From 8:00 to 9:00, Hoon studied for his physics test because he wanted to get a good grade. Then he took the bus to school because his car was in the garage. He met his friend Chen around 9:30. They studied in the library for an hour. At 11:00, Hoon had his physics test. After lunch, he had a French class from 1:00 to 3:00. For dinner, he went to see his friend Rachel. He cooked spaghetti, and she made a salad. From 7:00 to 9:00, they watched television. He got home about 9:30. Hoon studied for an hour and then went to bed.

1. (was) _Was Hoon studying for his test at 8:00 a.m.?_

2. (who) _____

3. (what) _____

4. (when) _____

5. (why) _____

6. (where) _____

7. (was) _____

8. (were) _____

9. (what) _____

B Find a partner and play a game. Ask your partner your questions. When you're answering, don't look at the paragraph. Count how many correct answers you and your partner have. Whoever answers the most questions correctly wins.

Lesson 40

Expansion Activity
Contrast: Past vs. Past Continuous Tenses

Name _____ Date _____

A Read the paragraph below. Circle the verbs in the past continuous tense. Underline the verbs in the past tense.

   When I <u>was</u> born, my family (was living) in a rural part of western Brazil. It was incredibly beautiful, but we were quite close to the jungle. One day, I was playing with my older brother in the backyard. We were digging holes in the ground and building castles with stones. While we were playing, I heard something behind me. I looked up and screamed. A jaguar was coming towards us slowly. Luckily, my grandmother was working in the garden with a big rake. She ran straight at the jaguar with the rake. It ran back into the jungle. Soon after that, we moved to a city.

B Write a true story about something scary or surprising that happened to you. Use the paragraph above as a model. Circle the verbs in the past continuous tense. Underline the verbs in the past tense.

Lesson 41

Expansion Activity
Verbs + Gerunds

Name _____ Date _____

A Complete the following sentences with your thoughts and opinions about health and exercising. Use a gerund after the verb. Then read your sentences to a partner.

1. My friends and I avoid *watching too much TV.*

2. People should consider _____

3. Most people dislike _____

4. I don't mind _____

5. My friends and I enjoy _____

6. I suggest _____

7. I can't imagine _____

8. I sometimes miss _____

9. People often put off _____

10. My parents recommend _____

11. Athletes should stretch when they finish _____

12. When I was a child, I practiced _____

13. Most days, I feel like _____

14. I should really quit _____

EXPANSION ACTIVITIES

LESSON 42

Expansion Activity
Expressions with Verbs + *-ing*

Name _____ Date _____

A Read each sentence. Use the expressions below + verb + **-ing** to write a new sentence that has a similar meaning. Use each of the expressions at least once. More than one answer is possible.

| spend + (amount of time) | have fun | have a good time | have a great time |
| have trouble | have a hard time | have problems | |

1. It was difficult for Ibrahim to find a good campsite.
   Ibrahim had a hard time finding a good campsite.

2. Nancy enjoyed camping.
   _____

3. Paloma tried to build a fire, but the wood was wet. The matches kept going out.
   _____

4. Ibrahim didn't sleep well on the hard ground.
   _____

5. It took Mathew four hours to find enough firewood.
   _____

6. It was difficult for Joshua to hike eight miles yesterday.
   _____

7. Barney really liked swimming in a mountain lake.
   _____

8. The car wouldn't start when they wanted to leave. Finally, Paloma figured out the problem.
   _____

9. Driving home took them six hours.
   _____

EXPANSION ACTIVITIES

Lesson 43

Expansion Activity
Gerund Subjects

Name _____ Date _____

A Join a group of two or three students, and make a guidebook for learning English. Write eleven sentences of advice. Begin each sentence with a gerund subject. Start three sentences with a negative gerund subject.

1. Studying at least a half hour every day is a good idea.
2. _____
3. _____
4. _____
5. _____
6. _____
7. _____
8. _____
9. _____
10. _____
11. _____
12. _____

EXPANSION ACTIVITIES

Lesson 44

Expansion Activity
Adjectives with *-ing* and *-ed*

Name _____ Date _____

A Read the paragraph below. Underline the correct adjective in the parentheses.

Betty,

　　I went to an (1. <u>amazing</u>/amazed) party last week. I met two very (2. interesting/ interested) people, Frank and Billy. Frank is a musician who plays the trumpet. He's a (3. fascinating/fascinated) man. He plays (4. exciting/excited) jazz that's really fast. He thinks slow jazz is (5. annoyed/annoying). I'm (6. amazing/amazed) by his energy. Billy is very different from Frank, as he is very (7. relaxing/relaxed). At the party, he looked as if he felt (8. boring/bored), but he didn't. I had a (9. stimulating /stimulated) conversation with him. He spends a lot of time reading and thinking. He thinks philosophy and literature are very (10. interesting/interested). For me, reading philosophy is really (11. boring/bored), but I loved listening to Billy talk about it.

　　Take care,
　　Francine

B Write a paragraph about someone you met recently. Use at least six adjectives with **-ing** and **-ed**.

_____
_____
_____
_____
_____
_____
_____

LESSON 45

Expansion Activity
Contrast: -ing Forms

Name _____ Date _____

A Complete the sentences below. Use the **-ing** form of the word in parentheses and a helping verb, if necessary.

1. Last week, I went to a workshop on careers in aviation. Now, I (think) __am thinking__ about becoming a pilot.

2. It was very crowded. People (stand) _____ at the back of the room.

3. A woman led the workshop. She said, "(Become) _____ a pilot is a great dream to have."

4. Everyone thinks that it's a very (excite) _____ job.

5. However, (be) _____ a pilot is difficult.

6. My uncle is a pilot. Right now, he (fly) _____ a route from Cleveland, Ohio to Atlanta, Georgia.

7. Before that, he (fly) _____ from Reno to Dallas.

8. When he was young, he lived in Paris. (Live) _____ in Paris again some day is his dream.

9. He loves (eat) _____ French food.

10. He only takes a few vacation days a year. He (work) _____ hard for his future.

11. Right now, his pilot job is quite (bore) _____.

B Write true sentences about your present career or a career that you are interested in. Use the **-ing** form in parentheses.

1. (gerund object) __I am considering becoming an engineer.__

2. (gerund subject) _____

3. (present continuous) _____

4. (gerund object) _____

5. (past continuous) _____

6. (adjective) _____

EXPANSION ACTIVITIES 45

LESSON 46

Expansion Activity

Verbs + Infinitives and Verbs + Objects + Infinitives

Name _____ Date _____

A Read the paragraph below. Underline all of the verbs + infinitives and verbs + objects + infinitives. Write **VI** above the verbs + infinitives. Write **VOI** above the verbs + objects + infinitives.

    When I was younger, my parents <u>wanted me to go</u> [VOI] to medical school. They saved up all of their money and planned to pay for my college. They expected me to study biology and chemistry. I followed their plan for one year, but then I told them that I hated science. I loved to read great literature, and I didn't want to be a doctor. I tried to convince them that being a doctor wasn't for me. They finally understood and allowed me to change my major. I am now a professor of literature at a small college in Oregon. I have a son. I want him to read great books, but he would like to be a doctor. My parents are very happy with him. I'm happy that he knows what he wants.

B Write a paragraph about your childhood or teenage ambitions. What did you want to be? What are you now? Include at least four verbs + infinitives and two verbs + objects + infinitives in your paragraph.

_____
_____
_____
_____
_____
_____
_____
_____

Lesson 47

Expansion Activity
Infinitives after Adjectives

Name _____ Date _____

A Write twelve true sentences about your experience learning to drive or learning to do something else. Make six of the sentences negative. Use the adjectives in parentheses before an infinitive.

1. (easy) *For me, it wasn't easy to learn how to drive.*

2. (lucky) _____

3. (afraid) _____

4. (ready) _____

5. (dangerous) _____

6. (happy) _____

7. (sad) _____

8. (important) _____

9. (impossible) _____

10. (fun) _____

11. (expensive) _____

12. (possible) _____

13. (difficult) _____

LESSON 48

Expansion Activity
Infinitives of Purpose

Name _____ Date _____

A Read the following letter to the advice column, *Dear Annie*. Underline all of the infinitives of purpose.

Dear Annie,

   I'm a good decision-maker when it comes to career choices, but when it comes to relationships and marriage, I need some help. I chose to come to Chicago <u>to find</u> a good job. Then I chose to study English to get an even better job. I chose to be a computer engineer to earn a lot of money. Now I have a really good job and am saving money to buy a house. My next big choice is about marriage. I'm seeing someone I really care about but am not sure if I should ask her to marry me. I know that you have to be really in love to propose to someone. I don't want to do it just to please my family or anyone else. Can you give me some advice?

   Confused in Chicago

B Write a letter to *Dear Annie* that is similar to the one above. What choices have you made in your life? Why did you make those choices? Did you make the right choices? Use five infinitives of purpose and underline them.

_____
_____
_____
_____
_____
_____
_____
_____
_____
_____

EXPANSION ACTIVITIES

Lesson 49

Expansion Activity
Verb + Infinitive or Gerund

Name _____ Date _____

A Joan and Lin are on a first date. Read their conversation below, and underline the gerunds and infinitives.

Joan: Do you like <u>going</u> to movies?

Lin: I love seeing movies! What kind do you like?

Joan: I like to watch Chinese movies the best, but I can't stand going to Chinese martial arts movies.

Lin: Really? Well, *Red Thunder* is playing at the Centerville Theater. It's not far from here. Let's start walking. It'll take about ten minutes.

Joan: Great idea! After the movie, let's go to dinner. What kind of food do you like?

Lin: Well, I recently started going to that new Thai place on Sutter Street. It's really good.

Joan: Thai food is OK, but I prefer eating French or Italian food.

Lin: OK, let's have Italian then. I love to eat pasta.

B Write a dialogue for two people on a first date. Use the verbs below. Write at least three sentences with verb + infinitive and three sentences with verb + gerund.

begin	continue	like	prefer
can't stand	hate	love	start

_____
_____
_____
_____
_____
_____
_____

EXPANSION ACTIVITIES

Expansion Activity
Phrasal Verbs 1 (Separable)

LESSON 50

Name _____ Date _____

A In the sentences below, separate the verb and particle with the pronoun form of the underlined noun phrase.

1. Motoki's boss passed out <u>a report in English</u> to the team.
   Motoki's boss passed it out to the team.

2. Motoki had to look over <u>the report</u> for his boss.

3. At first, he put off <u>reading the report</u>.

4. Then, he looked over <u>the many paragraphs in the report</u>.

5. He wrote down <u>the words that he didn't understand</u>.

6. He looked up <u>some difficult verbs</u> in a grammar book.

7. He finally figured out <u>the sentences</u>.

8. He handed in <u>his translation of the report</u> yesterday.

9. He found out <u>that the boss was very pleased with his translation</u> this morning.

10. Today, the boss handed out <u>a longer report in English</u>.

11. Motoki wants to give back <u>his Japanese translation</u> tomorrow.

LESSON 51

Expansion Activity
Phrasal Verbs 2 (Inseparable)

Name _____ Date _____

A Read the letter from an American high school student to a pen pal. Underline the inseparable phrasal verbs. Circle the object if there is one.

Dear Pen Pal,

   I <u>grew up</u> in a very small rural community. There wasn't much to do, but I had fun with my friends. I always got up early in the morning to help my mother make breakfast. On school days, I had to get on the bus around 7:00 in the morning and ride for ten miles. I got off in Dade City. I came back home around 3:30. My parents were still at work, so my grandmother looked after me. I often ate a snack and then dropped by a friend's house. It was a very small community, so we were always running into friends. I sometimes ate dinner at a friend's house. There were no restaurants in my community, so nobody ever ate out. My friends and I sometimes had no homework, so we stayed out until sunset. After dark, there wasn't anything to do, so I always just went back home.

                                            Sincerely,
                                            Mark

B Write a letter to Mark about your childhood. Talk about where you grew up and where you went to school. Use at least five inseparable phrasal verbs in your paragraph. Underline the phrasal verbs and circle the object if there is one.

_____
_____
_____
_____
_____
_____
_____

EXPANSION ACTIVITIES

Lesson 52

Expansion Activity
Verb + Preposition Combinations

Name _____ Date _____

A Find the mistakes. Rewrite the sentences. One sentence is correct.

1. In high school, I participated on many activities.
   In high school, I participated in many activities.

2. When I started high school, I was really looking forward to graduate.

3. I believed about the value of education, but I wanted to be free.

4. It was difficult for me to concentrate in my studies.

5. My father told me that I should care of my studies more.

6. He and my mother dreamed in having a doctor in the family.

7. I listened at their advice.

8. I started to concentrate on being a better student.

9. Now, I am starting to succeed on my classes.

10. I look forward to be a university student.

11. In the future, I will always depend about my parents for good advice.

EXPANSION ACTIVITIES

Lesson 53

Expansion Activity
Adjective + Preposition Combinations

Name _____ Date _____

A Jorge is applying for a job. Complete his application letter with the correct prepositions.

Dear Ms. Harrison:

    I am interested (1.) ___*in*___ the bookkeeper position at your company and would like to schedule an interview with you. I am now working for a small grocery store as a bookkeeper. I am excited (2.) _____ the idea of working for a larger company. In my current job, I am responsible (3.) _____ paying all of the bills and the employees' salaries. I am an excellent employee and am never late (4.) _____ work. I am very good (5.) _____ handling money. I was successful (6.) _____ cutting costs in the store, but I am capable (7.) _____ doing much more. I believe that I am perfect (8.) _____ the position. Please contact me at (869) 555-9520 to schedule an interview.

                                        Sincerely,

                                        Jorge Borges

B Write an application letter for a job that you would really like to have. Write at least five sentences that have an adjective + preposition combination.

Dear _____

_____
_____
_____
_____
_____
_____

                                        Sincerely,

                                        _____

LESSON 54

Expansion Activity
Could/May/Might (Possibility)

Name _____ Date _____

A Complete the dialogue below using **could**, **may**, or **might** and the words in parentheses.

Vic: Good afternoon, Patricia. Thanks for coming over for lunch.
Patricia: It's my pleasure. Where's Leonard?
Vic: I don't know. He was going to drive here. He's very late.
Patricia: There (1. be/traffic jam) _There could be a traffic jam._
Vic: I was driving around a little while ago. There didn't seem to be any problems. But he has a very old car.
Patricia: He (2. be/stuck/somewhere) _____
Vic: Yes, that's a possibility. But you know, I just moved here last month. He doesn't even know my new address.
Patricia: He (3. be/ at your old house) _____
Vic: Oh, I hope not. How will he find us?
Patricia: He (4. call/you/on his cell phone) _____
Vic: Yeah, that's what he'll probably do.
Patricia: (5. he/arrive/soon) _____
Patricia: Yes, you're right.
Vic: Look over there. Something strange is happening.
Patricia: What do you mean?
Vic: There's a man climbing into that window.
Patricia: That (6. be/his house) _____
Vic: Why doesn't he use the door?
Patricia: He (7. not/have/his key) _____
Vic: No, I know the people there. He doesn't live there.
Patricia: He (8. be/a burglar) _____
Vic: The police (9. come/soon) _____
Patricia: Yes, but let's call them anyway.

54 EXPANSION ACTIVITIES

Lesson 55

Expansion Activity
Must (Making Logical Conclusions)

Name _____ Date _____

A Complete the dialogue below with **must** or **must not** and a verb.

Sarah: I had a really interesting day. I walked around the city. In the morning, I walked by that new house on the corner. A family was moving furniture into it.

Jaime: They (1.) _must be_ the owners.

Sarah: That's what I thought. They have a lot of expensive furniture!

Jaime: They (2.) _____ rich.

Sarah: I agree. They were carrying in a lot of toys, too.

Jaime: They (3.) _____ children.

Sarah: I saw a lot of dolls and cute dresses, but nothing for boys.

Jaime: They (4.) _____ any sons.

Sarah: Then I went downtown. On Main Street, I saw Mary's store. Somebody broke the window in her pastry shop.

Jaime: Mary (5.) _____ really angry!

Sarah: Yes, she *is* really angry. And the person stole all of her best pastries.

Jaime: That person (6.) _____ pastries a lot!

Sarah: I think so, too.

Jaime: Did you see Mary's daughter?

Sarah: Yes, she looked really tired. She said that college is really difficult.

Jaime: She (7.) _____ a lot of homework!

Sarah: Yeah. She's always working.

Jaime: Well, you (8.) _____ tired after your busy day.

Sarah: Yes, I am. I'm going to rest. I'll talk to you later.

EXPANSION ACTIVITIES 55

LESSON 56

Expansion Activity
Should (Advice) and Have to (Necessity)

Name _____ Date _____

A Join a group of two or three students. Write a short guidebook with advice about going to your school. Use **should**, **shouldn't**, **have to**, and **don't have to**, at least once each.

1. You have to arrive early because there aren't many parking places.
2. _____
3. _____
4. _____
5. _____
6. _____
7. _____
8. _____
9. _____

B Find the mistakes. Rewrite the sentences. One sentence is correct.

1. My brother should to study harder.
   My brother should study harder.

2. He has to studies tonight because he has a test tomorrow.
   _____

3. My parents have talk to him about his studies.
   _____

4. I don't think that he should play so many video games.
   _____

5. He shoulds go to college because he is very intelligent.
   _____

Lesson 57

Expansion Activity
Questions with *Should* and *Have to*

Name _____ Date _____

A A high school student is talking to his mother about going to college. Write the mother's questions for her son. In items with underlined words, replace the underlined words with a question word.

1. Q: <u>When do you have to apply to colleges?</u>
   A: I have to apply to colleges <u>in the next two months</u>.

2. Q: _____
   A: I want to go to Central City College <u>because they have good science classes</u>.

3. Q: _____
   A: Yes, I should talk to the counselor at school.

4. Q: _____
   A: Yes, I have to get good grades this year.

5. Q: _____
   A: <u>My teachers and the counselor</u> have to write letters of recommendation for me.

6. Q: _____
   A: Yes, we should apply for financial aid soon.

7. Q: _____
   A: Yes, my friend Jose should apply to good schools because of his excellent grades.

8. Q: _____
   A: I have to get a job <u>to earn some money for college</u>.

9. Q: _____
   A: Yes, I'll have to live in the dormitory my first year.

10. Q: _____
    A: I have to get up <u>at 7:00</u> tomorrow morning. I have an important test tomorrow.

EXPANSION ACTIVITIES

LESSON 58

Expansion Activity
The Base Form of a Verb

Name _____ Date _____

A Complete the dialogue with the correct form of the verb in parentheses.

Dad: Mary, did you (1. have) __have__ a good day today?

Mary: Yes, Dad. I (2. have) _____ a really nice day.

Dad: Really? That (3. be) _____ great!

Mary: Yeah, I (4. run) _____ into Arnold in the park.

Dad: He (5. be) _____ such a nice man. Does he still (6. work) _____ at the bank?

Mary: No, he used to (7. work) _____ there, but he's a student now. He (8. study) _____ for a master's degree in business.

Dad: That's wonderful! He will (9. do) _____ really well. I should (10. call) _____ him to say, "Hi."

Mary: Well, he's going to (11. come) _____ over for dinner Saturday night.

Dad: I'm really happy to (12. hear) _____ that. You two used to (13. be) _____ such good friends in high school.

Mary: I know. I'm glad I ran into him. You know, it must (14. be) _____ difficult for him to (15. find) _____ time to study. He has to (16. work) _____ on the weekends.

Dad: I can't imagine (17. get) _____ a master's degree while working. But he's young! He'll (18. be) _____ OK! I'm really looking forward to (19. see) _____ him again!

Mary: Me, too.

Lesson 59

Expansion Activity
Present Perfect Tense

Name _____ Date _____

A Complete the sentences below with the present perfect form of the verb in parentheses.

1. Martha's mother and father (be married) _have been married_ for 25 years.

2. Martha's brother (climb) _____ Mount Everest twice.

3. Martha (live) _____ in five different countries.

4. Martha's sister (be) _____ the CEO of a large corporation.

5. Martha's grandmother (learn) _____ five languages.

6. Martha's grandfather (write) _____ three novels.

7. Martha's father (invent) _____ three machines.

8. Martha's family (do) _____ many remarkable things.

B Write six sentences about your family and friends. Use the present perfect tense. Then read your sentences to a partner.

1. _____

2. _____

3. _____

4. _____

5. _____

6. _____

EXPANSION ACTIVITIES

LESSON 60

Expansion Activity
Present Perfect Tense with *Since* and *For*

Name _____ Date _____

A Complete the letter below with **since** or **for**. Underline the verbs in the present perfect tense.

Dear Aunt Grace,

I'm really sorry that I haven't written you (1.) ___for___ so long. I have lived in Montreal, Canada (2.) _____ four years and my life here is really busy. When I first arrived, I studied English for a few months. After living in Canada for one year, I got a job at McKay Imports. I have worked for them (3.) _____ then. They liked my work a lot and promoted me. I have been a manager (4.) _____ two years. The company asked me to start an M.B.A. program at McGill University. I have taken night and weekend classes (5.) _____ a year and a half. Studying and working at the same time is difficult, but I really want the degree. I'm going to finish my M.B.A. next year.

I have known a wonderful Canadian man named Karl (6.) _____ two years. We have been married (7.) _____ last December. We bought a house in January and have lived in it (8.) _____ three months. We even bought a dog! We have had Fluffy (9.) _____ two weeks.

Do you remember my younger sister Kathy? She has lived with us (10.) _____ March. She has worked (11.) _____ last month as an accountant. She has studied English at night (12.) _____ she arrived.

We really love Canada, except for the winter, of course, and we hope that you'll visit us soon.

Sincerely,

Miranda

LESSON 61

Expansion Activity
Present Perfect Tense—Yes-No Questions With *Ever*, Statements with Frequency Adverbs and Expressions

Name _____ Date _____

A In the table below, write six questions for another student about exciting activities. Find a partner. Ask him or her the questions, and circle the answers in the table. When you answer the questions, use frequency adverbs and expressions.

Questions	Answers
Have you ever gone scuba diving?	Yes, I have. No, I haven't.
	Yes, I have. No, I haven't.
	Yes, I have. No, I haven't.
	Yes, I have. No, I haven't.
	Yes, I have. No, I haven't.
	Yes, I have. No, I haven't.
	Yes, I have. No, I haven't.

B Write your partner's answers on the lines below using complete sentences. Read your sentences to the class.

EXAMPLES:
Ted: *Ali has gone scuba diving twice.*
Ted: *Ali has never hiked a volcano.*

_____
_____
_____
_____
_____

EXPANSION ACTIVITIES

LESSON 62

Expansion Activity
Present Perfect Tense—Statements and Questions with *Yet* and *Already*

Name _____ Date _____

A Read the following conversation. Underline the verbs in the present perfect tense. Circle the short answers.

Jane: Jonas, <u>have</u> you <u>packed</u> your bags?

Jonas: (No, Mom, I haven't.) I'm going to do it tonight.

Jane: Have you bought a new suitcase?

Jonas: Yes, I have. It's right here.

Jane: It's beautiful, Jonas. Have you brought the old trunk up from the basement?

Jonas: Yes, I have. It's downstairs. I have to clean it this afternoon.

Jane: Have you told all of your friends your new address?

Jonas: Yes, I have. I told everyone at my going away party last night.

Jane: That's good. Has Dad bought you a bus ticket for tomorrow? He sometimes forgets things these days.

Jonas: Yes, Mom. He has. But he hasn't given me the address of his old friend in New York. He wanted me to visit him.

Jane: I'll remind him. His friend Andy can help you a lot when you first get there. Well, we'll miss you, son.

Jonas: I'll miss you too, Mom.

B Use **yet** in six present perfect questions about the conversation above. Write answers to the questions using **yet** and **already**.

1. Has Jonas packed his bags yet? No, he hasn't packed his bags yet.
2. _____
3. _____
4. _____
5. _____
6. _____
7. _____

62 EXPANSION ACTIVITIES

LESSON 63

Expansion Activity
Present Perfect Tense—Questions with *How many times* and *How long*

Name _____ Date _____

A Erik is interviewing Alice about surfing. Complete the conversation with **how many times**, **how long**, **for**, and **since**.

Erik: Alice, (1.) __how long__ have you been a surfer?

Alice: I've been a surfer (2.) _____ three years.

Erik: How did you learn to surf?

Alice: Well, at first I taught myself, but I've had a teacher (3.) _____ last year. That's helped a lot.

Erik: Where do you usually surf?

Alice: I usually go to Ocean Beach because there are always waves.

Erik: (4.) _____ have you surfed there?

Alice: I've surfed there (5.) _____ about two years.

Erik: (6.) _____ have you surfed at Mavericks?

Alice: I've gone there five times. I like it, but the waves are so huge that I usually just watch. I've only actually surfed there once.

Erik: This is a nice surfboard. (7.) _____ have you had it?

Alice: I've had it (8.) _____ two years. It's in bad condition now. I should buy another one for Hawaii. I'm going there next month.

Erik: (9.) _____ have you been to Hawaii?

Alice: I've never been there before. This will be my first time.

Erik: I'm sure it'll be exciting. (10.) _____ have you been to Florida?

Alice: I've been to Florida two times. It was quite lovely. My sister is there now.

Erik: (11.) _____ has she been there?

Alice: She has been there (12.) _____ February.

Erik: Well, it has been great talking to you.

EXPANSION ACTIVITIES

LESSON 64

Expansion Activity

Contrast: Past vs. Present Perfect Tenses

Name _____ Date _____

A Complete the letter below with the verb in parentheses in the past or the present perfect tense.

Dear Mom and Dad,

Things are going OK here in Barcelona. I (1. arrive) __arrived__ two weeks ago and (2. find) _____ a nice family to live with. I have a small room with a bath. The family doesn't speak English, so I (3. speak) _____ only Spanish with them so far. My school is on the other side of the city, so yesterday, I (4. buy) _____ a bus pass to get to school. School (5. not start) _____ yet, but I (6. make) _____ several friends already. Since I met my new friends, I (7. visit) _____ many beautiful places in the city with them. Two days ago, we (8. go) _____ to see a beautiful cathedral, and yesterday, we (9. drive) _____ with some friends to the beach. Two days ago, I (10. see) _____ Mario. Do you remember him? He (11. tell) _____ me to say, "Hello," to you. He (12. be) _____ an accountant for the Spanish government for a year now, but he doesn't really like his job. Well, I need to study some more. I'll write again.

Love,

Sophia

B Write a letter similar to the one above to someone you know. Describe your life now. Include at least three verbs in the past tense and three verbs in the present perfect tense. Circle the verbs in the past tense, and underline the verbs in the present perfect tense.

Dear _____,

_____

_____

_____

_____

_____

Sincerely,

_____

Review Test: Lessons 1–5

Name _____ Date _____

A Look at the underlined words in each sentence. Write **noun**, **verb**, **adjective**, **adverb**, or **preposition** in each blank.

EXAMPLE: ____adverb____ I drove to my office <u>carefully</u>.

1. _____ Carla won a <u>trip</u> to Hawaii.

2. _____ She learned English <u>fast</u>.

3. _____ She <u>wrote</u> an excellent composition.

4. _____ The weather was perfect <u>in</u> Hawaii.

5. _____ Her room was <u>comfortable</u> and quiet.

6. _____ She liked to sit <u>on</u> her balcony.

7. _____ She <u>went</u> to the beach every day.

8. _____ She met many wonderful Hawaiian <u>people</u>.

9. _____ Carla thinks Hawaiian culture is very <u>interesting</u>.

10. _____ She's happy that she studied <u>hard</u> and wrote a great composition.

B Find the mistakes. Rewrite the sentences.

EXAMPLE: Lin and I are goods students.
   Lin and I are good students.

1. My friend Lin and I are in school at 8:00 to 12:00.

2. Our teacher is kind man.

3. Our classes interesting.

4. We learn a lot for English.

5. We sometimes have homework difficult.

6. We try to do our homework good.

7. Some students not come to class every day.

8. Many student come to school every day.

9. Lin and I study hardly every day.

10. Our class ends in june.

Review Test: Lessons 6-9

Name _____ Date _____

A Find the mistakes. Rewrite the sentences.

EXAMPLE: Sam he goes to school every day in Chicago.

<u>Sam goes to school every day in Chicago.</u>

1. Is a very good job.
_____

2. He born in Russia 48 years ago.
_____

3. They very happy in Chile.
_____

4. My father he lives in China.
_____

5. This my brother.
_____

B Complete the sentences with the words below. More than one answer is possible, and words can be used more than once. Add commas if necessary.

| and | or | but | so | because |

EXAMPLE: Herbert is very handsome, ___<u>but</u>___ he's not a nice person.

1. Julia, Sophia _____ Louise are all going to the store.

2. Should we go to the Thai restaurant _____ eat at the Indian restaurant?

3. I don't want to go hiking _____ I hurt my foot last week.

4. I really like Martin _____ I don't like his sister at all!

5. Li has a lot of homework _____ she's not going to the party.

REVIEW TESTS 67

C Complete the sentences with the verb *BE* in the past, present, or future tense.

EXAMPLE: Mylo ___is___ a singer.

1. Mylo _____ born in a small village.

2. He and his family (not) _____ rich. They had a small farm.

3. When Mylo plays music at a concert, his wife and daughter _____ always with him.

4. His daughter _____ two years old next week.

5. He (not) _____ in Miami again soon.

D Look at the Charlie's daily schedule. Use the word in parentheses to combine the two sentences.

6:30 – eat breakfast	5:50 – change clothes
7:00 – go to work	6:15 – eat a snack
12:00 – eat lunch in park	7:00 – have dinner
12:30 – take a walk	7:30 – wash dishes
1:00 – go back to work	10:59 – finish reading
5:49 – get home	11:05 – go to sleep

EXAMPLE: (after) Charlie gets up. He eats breakfast.

   After Charlie gets up, he eats breakfast.

1. (after) Charlie eats lunch. He takes a walk.

2. (before) Charlie takes a walk. He goes back to work.

3. (when) Charlie changes his clothes. He gets home.

4. (before) Charlie eats a snack. He has dinner.

5. (after) Charlie finishes reading. He goes to sleep.

Review Test: Lessons 10–13

Name _____ Date _____

A Underline the correct words in parentheses.

1. Our neighbors (<u>make</u>/are making) a lot of noise every night. Their son (plays/is playing) the drums after dinner. He (plays/is playing) right now. I (think/'m thinking) about talking to his parents. My husband (disagrees/is disagreeing) with me. He (thinks/is thinking) the noise isn't a problem.

2. It's Saturday night, and Harry's restaurant (is/is being) almost empty! Usually, a lot of people (come/are coming) here on the weekends. But today, most people (listen/are listening) to music in the city park. Mylo (plays/is playing) a free concert right now. He often (gives/is giving) free concerts in the park.

B Complete the sentences with the correct past tense form of the verb.
EXAMPLE: Last year, I (decide) __*decided*__ to visit my girlfriend in Brazil.

1. I ([not] have) _____ a good trip.

2. First, I almost (miss) _____ my flight.

3. I (get) _____ to Brazil late at night.

4. My girlfriend (not, meet) _____ me at the airport.

5. She (forget) _____ that I was coming to see her!

6. I (call) _____ her on the phone.

7. She ([not] be) _____ at home.

8. I (leave) _____ a message.

9. I (wait) _____ two hours for her.

10. Finally, she (come) _____ to get me. After that, the vacation was much better!

C Rewrite these sentences about the past using **used to**.

EXAMPLE: In the past, people rode horses.

In the past, people used to ride horses.

1. Many men had long hair when my father was young.

2. Did people think that the world was flat a long time ago?

3. One hundred years ago, the people in this town never traveled during the winter.

4. People had a lot of children in the old days.

5. Was gas 25 cents a gallon when you were young?

6. My father can remember when people didn't have televisions in their homes.

7. Did your sister travel much when she was young?

8. I remember when it cost two dollars to see a movie.

9. When I was a kid, many people didn't wear seat belts.

10. Did the milkman deliver bottles of milk to your parents' house?

Review Test: Lessons 14–17

Name _____ Date _____

A Complete the sentences using the words(s) in parentheses with **be going to** or **will**.

EXAMPLE: Tamon: What (you, do) _are you going to do_ this afternoon?

1. Ivan: I (go) _____ to a party. How about you?

   Tamon: I want to go to the library, but it's raining. I need a ride.

2. Ivan: Don't worry. I (take) _____ you!

   Tamon: Thanks! I'm really worried about the test tomorrow.

3. Ivan: I'm sure that you (pass) _____ the test.

4. Tamon: Mary (meet) _____ me at the library at 6:30. We have a 7:00 reservation at a restaurant for dinner.

5. Ivan: I hope that she (be) _____ late.

   Tamon: She's always late!

6. Tamon: What (you, do) _____ tomorrow?

7. Ivan: You don't remember? We planned it last week. You, Mary, Rebecca, and I (have) _____ a picnic in the park tomorrow afternoon.

8. Tamon: Oh, yeah! Hey, Mary hates cigarettes, so please don't smoke at the picnic.

   Ivan: Don't worry. I (smoke) _____.

9. Tamon: Thanks! Uh, we should buy some food for the picnic.

   Ivan: Yeah, you're right.

   Tamon: (you, come) _____ to the supermarket with me tomorrow? We can get it done early, like 8:00.

10. Ivan: No, I (go) _____ that early. Tomorrow's Sunday. I want to sleep late. I'll go later.

B Circle the correct form of the verb in parentheses.

EXAMPLE: Alice is going to have a job interview. If Alice (gets/will get) the job, she will be happy.

1. Alice doesn't know what she (says/will say) if the interviewer (asks/will ask) about her job experience.

2. She (is going to eat/eats) something before she (goes/will go) to the interview.

3. After she (eats/will eat), Tom (will help/helps) her prepare for the interview.

4. Tom thinks that the interviewer (is/will be) impressed when he (meets/will meet) Alice.

5. When the interview (is/will be) finished, Alice (goes/will go) to the park.

C Look at Mary's schedule for next week. Write sentences with the present or present continuous about Mary's plans. Use the words in parentheses in your sentences.

Tuesday	Wednesday	Thursday	Friday	Saturday	Sunday
today	study for math test	visit parents	take math test		fly to New York departure-1 p.m. arrival-5 p.m.

EXAMPLE: (math test)

<u>On Wednesday, Mary is studying for her math test.</u>

1. (parents)

_____

2. (take math test)

_____

3. (fly to New York)

_____

4. (flight/leave)

_____

5. (arrive)

_____

Review Test: Lessons 18–20

Name _____ Date _____

A Complete the interview with Lee, an exchange student from Korea. Write **yes-no** questions for the answers.

EXAMPLE: Q: _Is this your first time in Australia?_
A: Yes. This is my first time in Australia.

1. Q: _____
   A: No. I wasn't born in China. I was born in Korea.

2. Q: _____
   A: Yes. I like Australian schools very much.

3. Q: _____
   A: Yes. At the end of the year, I'm going to travel around Australia.

4. Q: _____
   A: Yes. I made a lot of friends.

5. Q: _____
   A: Yes. I'm studying hard for final exams.

B John and Mandy are talking about Lee, the exchange student. Write a **Wh** question for each answer. Use the **Wh** word in parentheses.

EXAMPLE: Q: (where) _Where is Lee from?_
A: He is from China.

1. Q: (when) _____
   A: He came to Australia in September.

2. Q: (how) _____
   A: He likes our school a lot.

3. Q: (who) _____
   A: He is living with an Australian family now.

4. Q: (why) _____
   A: He came here because he wanted to experience another culture.

5. Q: (when) _____
   A: He'll return to China in September.

C Lee is complaining about his new roommate. Complete the sentences below with a form of the verb **do**.

EXAMPLE: My roommate ____doesn't____ help with the chores!

1. I asked him to _____ the dishes last night.

2. He _____ do them. The dirty dishes were still in the sink this morning.

3. Last week, I _____ all of the shopping.

4. Last night, I asked him, "_____ you do the laundry?" He said, "No."

5. I am not going to _____ all of the chores anymore.

D Find the mistakes. Rewrite the sentences.

1. People in this house don't doing their chores.
   _____

2. Ricardo didn't cleaned the bathroom.
   _____

3. When will Stephanie to do the dishes?
   _____

4. Who did wash the windows?
   _____

5. Makiko will to do the shopping tomorrow.
   _____

74 REVIEW TESTS

Review Test: Lessons 21–24

Name _____ Date _____

A Sherry is going to visit her family in Poland. Write questions with **How** or **Who** for the answers below.

EXAMPLE: Q: <u>Who is taking her to the airport?</u>

A: John is taking her to the airport.

1. Q: Who _____

    A: Sherry is going to go to Poland.

2. Q: How _____

    A: She is flying to Poland.

3. Q: How _____

    A: The flight is 15 hours.

4. Q: Who _____ stay with in Warsaw?

    A: She is going to stay with her aunt and uncle in Warsaw.

5. Q: Who _____ visit?

    A: She also wants to visit her grandmother.

6. Q: How _____

    A: Her grandmother's house is 50 miles from her aunt and uncle's house.

7. Q: How _____

    A: It takes about two hours to drive there.

8. Q: Who _____ with?

    A: She will visit her grandmother with her cousin Stan.

9. Q: How often _____

    A: Stan visits his grandmother once or twice a month.

10. Q: How _____

    A: His grandmother is doing very well.

REVIEW TESTS 75

B Complete the conversation below by making negative questions with **isn't**, **aren't**, **doesn't**, **don't**, or **didn't**.

EXAMPLE: Anna: Tony, why ____don't____ we watch some TV?

Tony: Anna, it's 10:00. (1) _____ your class start at 10:00?

Anna: No, (2) _____ I tell you? I moved to the 11:00 class.

Tony: Oh, that's right. Well, we have an hour. Why (3) _____ we go to the library? We can study.

Anna: (4) _____ the library closed now?

Tony: No, it opens at 9:00.

Anna: But (5) _____ your parents coming this morning?

Tony: Oh, no! I forgot. They're probably at my apartment now!

C Adam is interviewing his grandfather Chang. Write negative responses to each question. Use complete sentences.

EXAMPLE: Q: Did you have a happy childhood?
          A: _No. I didn't have a happy childhood._

1. Q: Did you grow up in Taipei?

   A: _____

2. Q: Could you speak Chinese when you were a child?

   A: _____

3. Q: Are you happy living in New York City?

   A: _____

4. Q: Are you working at a very important company?

   A: _____

5. Q: Are you going to visit your family in Taiwan soon?

   A: _____

Review Test: Lessons 25–28

Name _____ Date _____

A Martina and Alberto are in their garage. They are talking about their old things. Underline the correct word in parentheses.

EXAMPLE: Martina: What are you doing?
Alberto: I'm cleaning up (<u>our</u>/ours) garage.

Martina: What a mess! Oh, look over there! (1. Who's/Whose) old bicycle is that?
Alberto: That's (2. John's/Johns'). The other bicycle over there is (3. my/mine).
Martina: (4. It's/Its) in really bad shape.
Alberto: Yes, it is.
Martina: And look over there. There's a stack of magazines. Are they Mary's?
Alberto: Yes, they're (5. her's/hers). She left them here when she went to college.

B Sophie is looking for Mr. Kim because she needs to give him a report. Complete the sentences with the correct object pronoun.

EXAMPLE: Sophie: Yukio, I'm looking for Mr. Kim. Do you know where he is?
Yukio: I saw ____him____ a few minutes ago in the conference room.

Sophie: Thanks. I have a report for him. He needs (1.) _____ fast.

Yukio: Well, he's actually busy right now. Some people from France came to talk to (2.) _____.

Sophie: Is he meeting with (3.) _____ now?

Yukio: Yes. But maybe I can help (4.) _____. I'm going into the meeting now. Just give (5.) _____ the report. I'll give it to Mr. Kim.

Sophie: Thanks!

REVIEW TESTS 77

C Ellen is writing to her sister about her children. Complete the letter with the correct reflexive pronouns.

Dear Sue,

 I'm writing to you about Thanksgiving. I know that you and the kids want to come over for dinner. Honestly, I'm really worried about your kids. I'm sorry, but I have to talk to you about them. They help ___themselves___ to food and drinks without asking anyone. They also make a big mess. Ron and I have to clean it up. Last year, your son Harry fell down and hurt (1.) _____, and I was very upset. Ron and I can't enjoy (2.) _____ when they're running around the house. Every year, I tell (3.) _____ to just relax, but I can't. When you are at my house, I want you to make (4.) _____ at home, but you still have to control your kids. You must tell them to behave (5.) _____.

 Sincerely,
 Ellen

D Linda and Bob are talking about Bob's birthday party. Underline the correct indefinite pronoun in parentheses.

EXAMPLE: Linda: How did you like your birthday party?
 Bob: I loved it, and I think that (<u>everybody</u>/anybody) had a good time.

Linda: Yes, I agree. (1. No one/Anyone) complained.

Bob: Hey, did you hear about Tom going to Hong Kong?

Linda: No, I haven't heard (2. something/anything) about it. Tell me (3. everything/anything) that you know!

Bob: I'd be happy to, but first let's talk about food. I'm going to get some Chinese food right now. Are you hungry? Do you want me to get you (4. something/nothing)?

Linda: Sure. I could eat (5. nothing/anything)!

Bob: Great! I'll be right be back.

Review Test: Lessons 29–33

Name _____ Date _____

A Write **a**, **an**, or **Ø** in the blanks.

EXAMPLE: For our camping trip, we need to buy ___Ø___ batteries.

1. We'll need _____ flashlight, also.

2. Should we buy _____ sunscreen?

3. I think that we need _____ pillows.

4. I have _____ information about a good campground.

5. It may rain, so we should bring _____ umbrella.

B Circle the correct quantity word in parentheses.

EXAMPLE: I don't like Los Angeles. There is (much/(too much)) pollution there in the summer.

1. There aren't (some/any) museums in my hometown.

2. There aren't many cars, so there is only (a little/a few) air pollution.

3. My town has (so many/so much) beautiful scenery.

4. I love my hometown, but I live in Los Angeles because I can make (a lot of/too much) money here.

5. Sometimes I'm sad in Los Angeles because I have (any/no) friends here.

C Complete the sentences with **a**, **an**, **the**, or **Ø**.

EXAMPLE: Yesterday, I saw some mice in ___the___ kitchen.

1. Today, I saw _____ same mice in the living room.

2. Except for mice, I really love _____ animals.

3. This morning, there was _____ big bird outside my window.

4. I think the big bird was _____ owl.

5. _____ owl flew off after about an hour.

REVIEW TESTS

D Underline the correct word in parentheses.

EXAMPLE: My family lives in many different cities. I have two brothers. One lives in Beijing. (Another/<u>The other</u>) lives in Bangkok.

1. I have three sisters. One lives in Rio de Janeiro. (The others/The other) sisters live in Paris.

2. My family keeps getting bigger. My oldest sister has three children. She just told me that she is going to have (another/the other one) baby.

3. I have three brothers. One of my brothers has two children. (Another/The other) has three children.

4. My oldest sister has four children. One is a girl. (The other/The others) are boys.

5. My youngest sister has two children. She wants to have (the others/another one).

E Find the mistakes. Rewrite the sentences.

EXAMPLE: They have others friends.

<u>They have other friends.</u>

1. I don't like computer because they are not reliable.

_____

2. He went to library to get a book.

_____

3. Do they want another children?

_____

4. There is much crime in my city! It's dangerous here.

_____

5. He gave me an information about the statue and the bridge.

_____

Review Test: Lessons 34–37

Name _____ Date _____

A Write sentences with **as...as** or **not as...as** and the words in parentheses.

EXAMPLE: Maria has ten dollars. Jorge has ten dollars. (Maria/money)
   Maria has as much money as Jorge.

1. Maria is 20 years old. Jorge is 20 years old. (Maria/old)

_____

2. Maria's sports car isn't very safe. Jorge's minivan is very safe. (Maria's sports car/safe)

_____

3. Jorge drives fast. Maria drives fast. (Jorge/drive)

_____

4. Jorge's vacation in Hawaii cost $1,500. Maria's vacation in Paris cost $3,000. (Jorge's vacation in Hawaii/expensive)

_____

5. Hawaii was relaxing, but not exciting. Paris was really exciting. (Hawaii/exciting)

_____

B Underline the correct phrase in parentheses.

EXAMPLE: George wants to buy a new car. He has ten dollars. He (<u>doesn't have enough</u>/has too much) money.

1. Alberto lives near downtown. A man robbed him last week. He lost $75. Now he is afraid to go out at night. His neighborhood is (dangerous enough/too dangerous).

2. Yuriko lives in a big apartment. The rent is $2,000 a month. She makes $2,900 a month at her job. Her apartment is (expensive enough/too expensive).

3. Pierre and Helen have one child. They really want another child. They think that they (don't have enough/have too many) children.

4. Sally thinks people drive really fast near school. Herman agrees. He thinks that the people (don't drive fast enough/drive too fast).

5. Sam has a job at a factory. He earns $3,000 a month. He needs about $2,000 a month to pay his bills. Sam earns (enough money/too much money) to pay his bills.

REVIEW TESTS   **81**

C Use the comparative form of the adjective in parentheses to combine the sentences below.

EXAMPLE: Central City is really large. Bugville is really small. (large)
<u>Central City is larger than Bugville.</u>

1. Lee is really funny. Martin is serious. (funny)

2. Playing golf is good for your health. Swimming is excellent for your health. (good)

3. A sirloin steak is $15.00. A salad is $5.00. (expensive)

4. Martina's car is five years old. Sasha bought her car last week. (new)

5. Marcus is sometimes friendly. Tommy is always really friendly. (friendly)

D Look at the chart below. Use the superlative form of the words in parentheses to write five sentences about the colleges.

College Name	Casper College	Cogswell College	Jonesville College
Tuition	$5,000	$10,000	$25,000
Number of Students	25,000	15,000	5,000
Science Department	Good	Excellent	Very good
Dormitory Cost	$1,000 per year	$3,000 per year	$10,000 per year
Library	Medium	Large	Very large

EXAMPLE: (low tuition) <u>Casper College has the lowest tuition.</u>

1. (many students) _____

2. (good science department) _____

3. (high tuition) _____

4. (cheap dormitories) _____

5. (large library) _____

Review Test: Lessons 38–40

Name _____ Date _____

A Complete the sentences with the past continuous tense of the verbs in parentheses.

EXAMPLE: At noon, I (study) __was studying__ in the library.

1. Many students (read) _____ books.

2. After that, I went to the Student Union. A lot of people (play) _____ cards.

3. When I left, everyone (talk) _____ loudly.

4. The sun (shine) _____, and it was really warm.

5. A group of my friends (swim) _____ in the pool.

B A police officer is asking John about last night. Complete the questions using the past continuous and the question word in parentheses. When there is no question word, make a **yes-no** question.

EXAMPLE: police officer: (what) __What were you doing__ at 8:00 last night?

   John: I was sitting in the living room.

1. police officer: (what) _____ at that time?

   John: The maid was cleaning the library.

2. police officer: (who) _____ with her?

   John: Harry was talking with her.

3. police officer: (why) _____ to the maid?

   John: I don't know why Harry was talking with her.

4. police officer: _____ with her then?

   John: No, Martin wasn't talking with her then. He was in the kitchen at that time.

5. police officer: (when) _____ with her?

   John: Martin was talking with her later, around 9:00.

REVIEW TESTS   83

C Circle the correct words in parentheses.

EXAMPLE: I (went/was going) to an art opening last night. It was a wonderful party for a famous artist.

1. People (came/were coming) from all over the world.

2. The artist's plane (arrived/was arriving) late.

3. At 9:00, everyone (still waited/was still waiting) for her.

4. While the artist (riding/was riding) in the taxi from the airport, the people were eating. Then they started to go home.

5. When the artist finally (got/was getting) there, the food and the people were gone.

D Find the mistakes. Rewrite the sentences.

EXAMPLE: The phone rang while Harry took a bath.

The phone rang while Harry was taking a bath

1. Why Chen was studying for a test last night?
_____

2. Was the children doing their homework when their father came home?
_____

3. At 7:30 in the morning, everyone still slept.
_____

4. While Mary driving, Andrew was looking out the window.
_____

5. While Mr. Jang was cooking dinner, while the children watched TV.
_____

Review Test: Lessons 41–45

Name _____ Date _____

A Read the paragraph below. Underline all of the gerunds.

    Marianne is a student at a community college in New Jersey. She is living in a small town in central New Jersey. <u>Living</u> in New Jersey is very exciting for her. She can go to New York City on the weekends, and she enjoys <u>being</u> near farms and fields during the week. She likes her town because her neighbors are nice, and there isn't much crime or pollution. She dislikes <u>taking</u> the long bus ride to school every day, but her classes are all interesting. <u>Studying</u> computer programs is difficult for Marianne, but she likes <u>trying</u> to understand difficult things. She is having problems <u>learning</u> English right now, but she has a good time <u>talking</u> with students from many different countries in her English class. Her best friend Olivia is from the Czech Republic and is studying math. Marianne was thinking about <u>staying</u> in the United States after graduation, but <u>returning</u> to her country seems like a better idea now. She is having a hard time <u>being</u> away from her family so much. She likes <u>going</u> home during vacations, but it's not enough.

B Underline the correct word or phrase in parentheses.

EXAMPLE: I didn't really like the party last night. Most of the time, I was (boring/<u>bored</u>).

1. There was some (exciting/excited) music, but nobody danced.

2. The people talked about (boring/bored) subjects, like football.

3. The discussions about politics weren't (interesting/interested).

4. Most people seemed (relaxing/relaxed).

5. They may just have been (tiring/tired).

6. The best part of the party was the food. Martina brought an (amazing/amazed) garlic soup.

7. Mark told a (frightening/frightened) story about a burglary in the neighborhood.

8. Henry was (embarrassing/embarrassed) because he dropped a big bowl of potato chips on the carpet.

9. The hostess wasn't (annoying/annoyed), however. She just vacuumed up the chips.

10. There were a lot of nice people at the party, but I was still (disappointing/disappointed).

C Complete the sentences with a word or phrase from the box below.

| interesting | ~~am taking~~ | working |
| bored | was working | am graduating |

EXAMPLE: I ____am taking____ a class in elementary education.

1. The class is very _____.

2. The teacher makes the class very active, so I'm never _____.

3. Last semester, I _____ as an intern in an elementary school.

4. I _____ this semester, so I'll start looking for a teaching job very soon.

5. _____ as a teacher will be a fantastic career

Review Test: Lessons 46–49

Name _____ Date _____

A Underline the infinitives in the letter below.

Dear Ms. Johnston,
    Thank you for your nice letter. Yes, your son John arrived safely. He is happy <u>to be</u> here in Los Angeles. He has a very active life. He likes to hike in the Rocky Mountains. He started to take classes in scuba diving last month. He wants to go to San Diego in December to dive. He enjoys most sports. I will tell him to write you a long letter this weekend.
                                              Martina

B Underline the correct words in parentheses. If both answers are correct, underline both answers.

EXAMPLE: Last month, my son started (<u>to live</u>/<u>living</u>) in Montreal.

1. He went to Canada (to attend/attending) a good university.

2. Now, he's having a hard time (to study/studying).

3. He enjoys (to have/having) fun at night with friends.

4. He avoids (to attend/attending) classes that he doesn't like.

5. He doesn't like (to do/doing) his homework.

6. My wife and I are very worried that he will start (to get/getting) bad grades.

7. We want him (to succeed/succeeding) in his studies.

8. He plans (to go/going) to medical school after he gets his degree.

9. He will have to start (to work/working) much harder.

10. You have to be a good student (to get/getting) into medical school.

C Find the mistakes. Rewrite the sentences. One sentence is correct.

EXAMPLE: I'm studying business for to work for my mother's consulting company.

<u>I'm studying business to work for my mother's consulting company</u>

1. She often needs hiring new employees.

2. She enjoys to work with people.

3. It is sometimes difficult work such long hours.

4. She often works on weekends for get more business.

5. My mother is able increasing the number of her customers.

6. She told me to study marketing to learn about business.

7. She planned to visited me at my university.

8. She would like see me again.

9. I am considering to go home for Christmas.

10. I can't wait for seeing her again.

Review Test: Lessons 50–53

Name _____ Date _____

A Rewrite the sentences below. Replace the underlined words with a pronoun.

EXAMPLE: I try to turn in <u>my homework</u> on time.
   <u>I try to turn it in on time.</u>

1. The teacher handed out <u>the assignment</u>.
   _____

2. We all looked over <u>the math problems</u>.
   _____

3. I had to put off <u>doing my homework</u> because of my job.
   _____

4. The teachers let us make up <u>late work</u>.
   _____

5. The teacher called on <u>Ray</u> five times.
   _____

B Complete the sentences with one of the words below. Use each word only once.
   in   of   by   ~~down~~   with   about   into   over   out   to

EXAMPLE: I am careful to write ____down____ financial numbers correctly.

1. My boss used to look my figures _____ closely every day at 5:00.

2. She found _____ that I was doing a really good job.

3. I succeeded _____ earning her trust.

4. Now she is talking _____ promoting me to a better job.

5. I look forward _____ having more responsibility and a better salary.

6. She thinks that I am capable _____ being a store manager someday.

7. She knows that I get along _____ my co-workers.

8. I ran _____ my old friend John last week.

9. He wasn't surprised _____ my success.

REVIEW TESTS   **89**

C Find the mistakes. Rewrite the sentences. One sentence is correct.

EXAMPLE: Imelda is looking forward about changing jobs.
           Imelda is looking forward to changing jobs.

1. She is tired of to work for a low salary.

2. She is now responsible for train new employees.

3. Imelda hands training manuals out.

4. New employees need information, and Imelda looks up it for them.

5. Imelda is good to her job, but she is bored.

6. In the past, Imelda was afraid at looking for a new job.

7. She believes in work hard to succeed in life.

8. She is interested for getting a more challenging job.

9. She just got a new job at a company that is famous to make computers.

10. Imelda will certainly succeed in reach her goals.

Review Test: Lessons 54–58

Name _____ Date _____

A Complete the dialogue with **could, may, might, must, should, shouldn't, have to,** or **don't have to**.

Brad: Are you ready for the camping trip?

Brandi: Almost. I have everything on the bed, but I still ___have to___ put it in my backpack.

Brad: Did you bring warm clothes? It (1.) _____ be cold tonight. We'll be in the mountains.

Brandi: Yes, I did. Are you ready?

Brad: I'm packed, but now I have a headache.

Brandi: You (2.) _____ take an aspirin. It always helps me.

Brad: You're right. Hey, where's Harry? He's late.

Brandi: Yeah, he left his house an hour ago. There (3.) _____ be a lot of traffic.

Brad: Well, I hope he gets here soon. I want to leave on time.

Brandi: You (4.) _____ worry so much. We'll be just fine.

Brad: OK. I'll relax. Hey, don't let me forget. We have almost no gas in the van. We (5.) _____ stop at a gas station.

Brandi: OK. Oh, look. Harry just got here!

B Two parents are talking about their son. Write the mother's questions in the blanks. If there are underlined words, replace them with a question word.

EXAMPLE: Q: <u>Should we buy Tommy a new bicycle?</u>
A: Yes, we should. Tommy really needs a new bicycle.

1. Q: _____
   A: We should buy it at <u>Morgan's Department Store</u>.

2. Q: _____
   A: No, we don't have to pay cash. I can use my credit card.

3. Q: _____
   A: Yes, we have to buy it today. There's a big sale.

4. Q: _____
   A: We should give Tommy the bike <u>this Tuesday</u> since it's his birthday.

5. Q: _____
   A: No, we shouldn't drive to the store in your car. It's too small. The bike won't fit in it.

C Complete the dialogue with the correct form of the verb in parentheses.

EXAMPLE: Hey Martin, how (be) ___are___ you?

Martin: I'm doing fine, Brandi. Did you and your friends (1. go) _____ camping?

Brandi: Yeah. But we had to (2. find) _____ a new campground. Pinewoods Park is closed now.

Martin: That's too bad. We used to (3. have) _____ a lot of fun there.

Brandi: I really enjoyed (4. hike) _____ there. But Harp's Meadow is open. Let's go there today.

Martin: I'd like to go there today, but I (5. help) _____ my mom clean the house right now.

D Find the mistakes. Rewrite the sentences. One sentence is correct.

EXAMPLE: We had to fixed up our house.
We had to fix up our house.

1. It used to being a really nice house.

   _____

2. We had to did a lot of repair work.

   _____

3. My husband didn't took care of himself.

   _____

4. He must just be unlucky!

   _____

5. He hurt himself and may to be in the hospital for a week.

   _____

Review Test: Lessons 59–61

Name _____ Date _____

A Write the past participle form of each verb below.

EXAMPLE: work ___worked___

1. eat _____   2. go _____   3. learn _____
4. be _____   5. have _____

B Read the statements below about Joy. Write a sentence with a similar meaning using a verb in the present perfect tense.

EXAMPLE: Joy moved to Hawaii three years ago. She still lives there.
   Joy has lived in Hawaii for three years.

1. She was married. She is not married now.
   _____

2. When she was a child, she went skiing.
   _____

3. She started working for Federal Accounting one year ago. She still works there.
   _____

4. She visited Paris a long time ago.
   _____

5. Joy moved from an apartment to a house two years ago. She still lives in the house.
   _____

C Complete the sentences with **since** or **for**.

EXAMPLE: Abe and Joy have known each other ___for___ eight years.

1. They have been close friends _____ last year.
2. Abe has lived in Hawaii _____ December.
3. Abe has worked as a carpenter _____ ten years.
4. Joy has been an accountant _____ she graduated from college.
5. Abe has been sick _____ two days.

REVIEW TESTS 93

D Use the present perfect with **ever** to write questions for the answers below.

EXAMPLE: <u>Has Abe ever taught woodworking?</u>

Yes, he has. Abe taught woodworking in a high school for one year.

1. _____

   No, he hasn't. Abe doesn't know anything about sports, so he can't teach it.

2. _____

   Yes, they have. Abe and Joy love China. They went there twice last year.

3. _____

   No, they haven't. They're both afraid to go scuba diving.

4. _____

   Yes, she has. Joy often goes hiking.

5. _____

   Yes, they have. They ate Japanese food last week.

E Find the mistakes. Rewrite the sentences. One sentence is correct.

EXAMPLE: Eleanor and I have been in the United States since six years.

<u>Eleanor and I have been in the United States for six years.</u>

1. Has Eleanor's father visited ever you?

   _____

2. Yes, he has two times come to our house.

   _____

3. We have seen my parents rarely since we moved here.

   _____

4. We have lived in the same city for two years.

   _____

5. I have went back to my country only twice.

   _____

Review Test: Lessons 62–64

Name _____ Date _____

A Complete the conversation with **yet** or **already**.

EXAMPLE: Todd, have you done your homework ___yet___?

Todd: Yes, I've (1.) _____ done my homework. But I haven't done my chores (2.) _____.

Mother: Why haven't you done your chores (3.) _____?

Todd: I haven't had time. Has Mary come back from the store (4.) _____?

Mother: Yes, she's (5.) _____ gotten back. She came back an hour ago.

B Underline the correct words in parentheses.

Martha: John, (1. how many times/<u>how long</u>) have you lived here?

John: I've lived here for three years.

Martha: What do you do?

John: I'm a flight attendant. I work on jets flying to Europe.

Martha: Really? (2. How many times/How long) have you flown to Paris?

John: I've gone to Paris more times than I can count! I just got back from Paris yesterday.

Martha: That's incredible! I've only been to Paris (3. twice/ever).

John: It *is* really nice to go to Europe so often, but I'm actually very tired of my job.

Martha: (4. How many times/How long) have you been a flight attendant?

John: (5. Since I moved here./Since three years.) What do you do, Martha?

Martha: I'm a criminal lawyer. I just graduated from law school last year.

John: That must be exciting! (6. How many times/How long) have you gone to court?

Martha: I've gone to court ten times. It's interesting, but it's stressful!

C Use the verb in parentheses in the past or present perfect tense to complete the sentences.

EXAMPLE: Raoul, you're back! How (be) ____was____ your vacation?

Raoul: It was great! I (1. see) _____ all of my relatives in Nicaragua.
Kim: I'd love to go there. I (2. [not] ever be) _____ to Central America.
Raoul: You should go. You (3. study) _____ Spanish last semester, right?
Kim: Yes. I (4. take) _____ three Spanish classes since I started studying at this school.
Raoul: Wow, that's great. Where (5. go) _____ for your vacation?
Kim: I didn't go anywhere. I stayed here in Indianapolis. My aunt and uncle visited me.

D Write questions for the answers.

EXAMPLE: Q: _Have you finished the report yet?_
A: No, I haven't finished the report yet.

1. Q: _____

   A: I haven't finished it because Albert hasn't given me the information about expenses.

2. Q: _____

   A: I've needed that expense information for three days.

3. Q: _____

   A: Yes, I have. I asked him for the information a week ago.

4. Q: _____

   A: Yes, he did give me some information yesterday. It was next year's budget, not the expenses for last year.

5. Q: _____

   A: He has been late with important information four times this year. It's a big problem for me.

Student Book Answer Key

Getting to Know You: Student Book

A

Is this your first time at this school?	Are you happy today?	Do you work?	Do you like your job?	Do you like grammar?
Do you want a lot of homework?	Are you afraid of tests?	Do you want a vacation?	Do you understand TV shows in English?	Do you ever listen to the radio in English?
Do you know how to use a computer?	Do you have an email address?	Do you know other students in this class?	Do you have a good dictionary?	Do you like to play games?

Introduction: Student Book

A
Imagine
Chart
Sentence
Team
Match
Unscramble
Pretend
Clause
Timeline
Check
Phrase
Paragraph
Parentheses
Turns

Secret Message: Good luck learning English grammar!

Lesson 1: Student Book

A
Welcome back to Academy High School! I hope you had a good vacation. I have a few announcements. First, pick up your schedules in the office. Second, don't forget that our school is closed next Monday for Labor Day. Third, I have some very exciting news. Last week, Carla Matos won a prize for her wonderful composition. She and three other winners are going on a trip to Hawaii for two weeks in December. The teachers are all very proud of Carla. We are having a party for her today and everyone is invited. OK now, before I end my announcements, are there any questions?

STUDENT BOOK ANSWER KEY **97**

B

Proper nouns	Singular nouns	Plural nouns
1. Academy High School	7. vacation	15. announcements
2. Monday	8. office	16. schedules
3. Labor Day	9. school	17. winners
4. Hawaii	10. week	18. weeks
5. December	11. prize	19. teachers
6. Carla	12. composition	20. questions
	13. trip	
	14. party	

Lesson 2: Student Book

A

Dear Everyone,

　　I'm having a <u>wonderful</u> time. The weather is <u>perfect</u>. It's <u>hot</u> and <u>sunny</u> in the afternoon, but at night it gets <u>cool</u>. I swim and rest all day. I feel so <u>happy</u> here!

　　My hotel room is very <u>comfortable</u> and <u>quiet</u>, and I have a <u>beautiful</u> view of the beach. I love to sit on my balcony and watch the <u>huge</u> waves. And the food is <u>delicious</u>, especially the <u>fresh</u> pineapple. As you know, Hawaii is <u>famous</u> for pineapple.

　　I love Hawaii! I was <u>lucky</u> to win this <u>exciting</u> trip.

　　　　　　　　　　　　　　See you soon!
　　　　　　　　　　　　　　Love, Carla

B

1. __ Carla had a wonderful <u>vacation</u>.
2. ✓ It was a very <u>exciting</u> trip.
3. __ She went <u>swimming</u> every day.
4. __ They <u>traveled</u> by plane.
5. ✓ She wasn't <u>homesick</u>.
6. ✓ They visited some <u>interesting</u> sights.
7. ✓ The beach was <u>crowded</u>.
8. ✓ She wasn't <u>disappointed</u> in her trip.

C

1. Hawaii is very beautiful.
2. The food is delicious.
3. Carla has a very comfortable room.
4. She is having a wonderful vacation.
5. Her boyfriend is handsome.
6. In Hawaii the waves are very big.
7. Hawaii is famous for coffee.
8. There are many expensive stores.
9. It is a wonderful place.

D

　　My <u>favorite</u> place is <u>famous</u> for <u>tall</u> buildings. The streets are very <u>noisy</u> and <u>crowded</u>. Some of the restaurants are very <u>expensive</u>. The weather is <u>cold</u> in the winter and <u>hot</u> in the summer. Many <u>famous</u> people live in this place.

　　This place is New York City.

Lesson 3: Student Book

A

Mika: Excuse me, does the M bus <u>stop</u> here?
John: Yes. I'm <u>waiting</u> for the same bus. It sometimes <u>comes</u> a little late.
Mika: I don't <u>know</u> the bus schedule because I usually <u>drive</u>.
John: Well, I <u>hope</u> the bus <u>comes</u> soon. My class <u>starts</u> in 15 minutes! Professor Fields <u>hates</u> it when we<u>'re</u> late.
Mika: <u>Are</u> you in Mr. Field's English class?
John: Yes, I <u>am</u>. He<u>'s</u> a great teacher. I <u>like</u> him very much.
Mika: He <u>was</u> my teacher last year. I <u>liked</u> him, but he <u>gave</u> us a lot of homework.
John: He <u>gives</u> us a lot of homework, too. Oh, here<u>'s</u> the bus. Maybe I won't <u>be</u> late!

B

	Helping Verb	Main Verb
1. I'm studying English.	'm	studying
2. I came here last year.	Ø	came
3. We're waiting for the bus.	're	waiting
4. I don't own a car.	don't	own
5. Are you taking an English class?	are	taking
6. We aren't in the same class.	Ø	aren't
7. The class ends at 9:00 p.m.	Ø	ends
8. Do you need a ride home?	do	need

C

	Main Verb	Adjective
1. Jo usually <u>drives</u>.	✓	—
2. He's a <u>serious</u> student.	—	✓
3. He doesn't <u>need</u> a ride home today.	✓	—
4. We're very <u>busy</u> with school and work.	—	✓
5. Are you <u>married</u>, Mika?	—	✓
6. Can we <u>study</u> together sometime?	✓	—
7. What time does the bus <u>come</u>?	✓	—
8. She's not <u>worried</u> about her classes.	—	✓

Lesson 4: Student Book

A
HELP WANTED
Babysitter
We need a babysitter to pick up our daughter from school. We want someone who has a car and drives (1. careful/**carefully**). Call Linda at 555-2054.

Receptionist
We need someone who speaks English (2. good/**well**). Many of our customers are from other countries, so we want someone who can speak (3. slow/**slowly**) and (4. clear/**clearly**). Call Peter at 555-3752.

Secretary
We need someone who can speak English (5. fluent/**fluently**). We want a (6. **fast**/fastly) worker who can work (7. good/**well**) with other people. We want someone who types (8. **fast**/fastly)—at least 70 words per minute. Call Mike at 555-2303.

B

Adverb	Verb	Adverb	Verb
1. carefully	drives	5. fluently	speak
2. well	speaks	6. well	work
3. slowly	speak	7. fast	types
4. clearly	speak		

<u>　fast　</u>　　<u>worker</u>

D

1. He works ~~good~~ <u>well</u>.
2. He does ~~well~~ his homework <u>well</u>.
3. I am a <u>good</u> worker ~~good~~.
4. Do you speak <u>English</u> fluently ~~English~~?
5. We work <u>hard</u> ~~hardly~~ every day.
6. She holds the baby <u>carefully</u> ~~careful~~.

Lesson 5: Student Book

A

Anna: Joe! Where are you? I'm so worried (1.) <u>about</u> you. I heard the news (2.) <u>about</u> the accident (3.) <u>on</u> the radio.
Joe: I'm fine, but the traffic isn't moving.
Anna: I heard that a truck went (4.) <u>through</u> the tunnel in the wrong direction and hit a lot of cars.
Joe: That's right. I was driving (5.) <u>over</u> the bridge when the accident happened.
Anna: I'm glad you're OK. Listen, we have a meeting (6.) <u>with</u> Amy's teacher (7.) <u>at</u> 7 o'clock.
Joe: I know. Can you go (8.) <u>to</u> the meeting without me?
Anna: OK, but maybe you can come later. It's (9.) <u>in</u> Room . . .
Joe: Wait. I need to find a piece (10.) <u>of</u> paper. OK. Go ahead.
Anna: It's in Room 252. It's (11.) <u>on</u> the second floor of Building E.
Joe: And what's the name (12.) <u>of</u> Amy's teacher? I forgot!

B

1. <u>P</u>　I'm still <u>in</u> the car.
2. <u>T</u>　The meeting starts <u>at</u> 7:00.
3. <u>M</u>　We need to go <u>to</u> the meeting.
4. <u>O</u>　I don't want to miss the meeting <u>with</u> the teacher.
5. <u>M</u>　It was impossible to get <u>through</u> the tunnel.
6. <u>M</u>　Nobody could get <u>over</u> the bridge.
7. <u>O</u>　His wife heard the news <u>on</u> the radio.
8. <u>O</u>　He wrote the room number on a piece <u>of</u> paper.

C

1. Joe started <u>in</u> Baytown.
2. He drove <u>from</u> Baytown <u>to</u> Sandberry.
3. He drove <u>through</u> a tunnel.
4. There was a terrible accident <u>in</u> the tunnel.
5. Then he drove <u>over</u> a bridge.
6. Finally, he went <u>around</u> the corner by his house.
7. He got home <u>at</u> 7:00 p.m.

D

Last year I took a trip (with) my grandfather. We got (up) really early (in) the morning and drove six hours (from) our farm (to) Iowa City. We didn't stay (on) the highway. We drove (on) country roads and went (over) some beautiful, old one-lane bridges. There was nothing (on) the radio, so I was glad we had some CDs. We listened (to) a lot (of) country music (during) the trip. When we arrived (in) Iowa City, we weren't happy (about) the traffic and noise, but we stayed (at) my aunt's house (for) five days and had a good time.

Review Lessons 1–5: Student Book

A

Melissa works with children at a school in New York. She arrives early and spends six hours a day with the kids. She teaches them numbers and the letters of the alphabet. When the children are tired, she reads them stories. They sit quietly and listen. When the children don't behave well, Melissa talks to them. When it is necessary, she calls their parents. Her job as a teacher can be hard, but she's very happy.

B

Nouns	Verbs	Adjectives	Adverbs	Prepositions
Melissa	works	six	early	with
children	arrives	tired	quietly	at
school	spends	necessary	well	in
New York	teaches	hard		of
hours	are	happy		to
day	reads			
kids	sit			
numbers	listen			
letters	behave			
alphabet	talks			
stories	is			
parents	calls			
job	be			
teacher				

C

1. Johnny is <u>a</u> smart little boy.
2. He's ~~a~~ smart.
3. Johnny is an <u>athletic</u> boy ~~athletic~~.
4. Johnny and his twin sister Carol are ~~intelligents~~ <u>intelligent</u>.
5. They <u>are</u> excited about school.
6. Carol draws ~~careful~~ <u>carefully</u>.
7. She also sings ~~beautiful~~ <u>beautifully</u>.
8. They write their names ~~good~~ <u>well</u>.
9. She has two book<u>s</u> about dogs.
10. They are in school ~~at~~ <u>from</u> 9 a.m. to 3 p.m.
11. Their classroom is ~~in~~ <u>on</u> the second floor.
12. They are ~~children~~ very happy <u>children</u>.

D Possible answers:

School started (1.) <u>on</u> September 8th. Melissa was very (2.) <u>nervous/worried</u> because she wanted to do (3.) <u>well</u>. She wanted the (4.) <u>children</u> to like her.

When she (5.) <u>met/saw</u> the children, she (6.) <u>smiled/waved</u> and said, "Hi everyone. Welcome to kindergarten. My (7.) <u>name</u> is Melissa and I am your (8.) <u>teacher</u>."

When he heard this, a/an (9.) <u>crying/unhappy</u> (10.) <u>child/student</u> walked (11.) <u>to</u> the door very (12.) <u>quickly/fast</u>. He said, "I (13.) <u>want/have/need</u> to go home!" Melissa went to him and said, (14.) <u>"Don't worry. It's going to be all right."</u>

Have Fun Lessons 1–5: Student Book

Noun	Verb	Adjective	Adverb
beauty	------	beautiful	**beautifully**
a teacher	**teach**	------	------
an assignment	**assign**	------	------
an announcement	announce	------	------
comfort	comfort	**comfortable**	comfortably
a crowd	crowd	**crowded**	------
excitement	excite	excited/exciting	excitedly
a winner	**win**	------	------
a decision	**decide**	decisive	decisively
an owner	**own**	------	------
------	------	busy	**busily**
a marriage	marry	married	------
the beginning	**begin**	------	------
hunger	------	**hungry**	hungrily
------	------	nervous	**nervously**

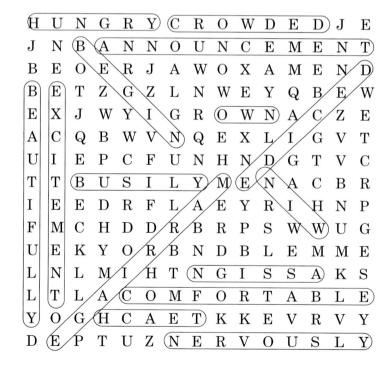

Lesson 6: Student Book

A

This <u>is</u>[S] my sister May. She <u>lives</u>[S] with my parents in Toronto. I[S] <u>don't see</u> her very often. We[S] <u>send</u> email to each other every day. She <u>works</u>[S] in a hospital as a nurse. It[S]<u>'s</u> a very good job. But it[S]<u>'s</u> not easy.

And these <u>are</u>[S] my grandparents. They[S] <u>came</u> to Canada many years ago. They <u>don't speak</u>[S] English well. Life in Toronto <u>is</u>[S] difficult for them.

B

(1.) <u>This</u>(is)my brother Li. (2.) <u>He/Li</u>(lives)in California. (3.) <u>He/Li</u>('s) married. His wife's name(is)Karen. (4.) <u>Karen/She</u>(comes)from Mexico. My brother and his wife(are)very happy. (5.) <u>They</u>(have)a beautiful daughter. (6.) <u>She</u>(is)almost a year old. (7.) <u>It</u>(')s her birthday next week.

	No Subject	No Verb	Two Subjects
1. It is hot today.	X		
2. My parents ~~they~~ live in New York.			X
3. My sister ~~she~~ has a job at a bank.			X
4. She is happy.		X	
5. It is a very good job.	X		
6. This is my brother.		X	
7. These are my parents.		X	

Lesson 7: Student Book

A

Dear Annie,

I have a problem. I have two boyfriends, Mark (1.) <u>and</u> John. Mark is handsome, (2.) <u>but</u> he isn't very nice to me. For example, last week I got angry at him (3.) <u>because</u> he didn't remember my birthday.

My other boyfriend is John. He isn't very handsome, (4.) <u>but</u> he is very kind to me. Last week he called me, took me to an expensive restaurant, (5.) <u>and</u> sent me flowers. I like him a lot, (6.) <u>but</u> I'm really in love with Mark.

Last week both Mark (7.) <u>and</u> John invited me to the senior dance. Should I go with Mark (8.) <u>or</u> John?

B

	Connecting Word	What is Being Connected
1. I have two boyfriends, Mark and John.	and	nouns
2. Mark is handsome, but he isn't nice to me.	but	sentences
3. He didn't call me or send me a present.	or	verbs
4. He didn't call me because he was busy.	because	sentences
5. He didn't call me, so I got angry at him.	so	sentences
6. I'm beautiful, smart, and funny.	and	adjectives
7. Should I go to the dance or stay home?	or	verbs
8. Should I go with Mark or John?	or	nouns
9. I can't decide, so I'll probably stay home.	so	sentences

Lesson 8: Student Book

A

Interviewer:	So Mylo, tell me about your childhood. (1.) <u>Were you</u> born in Mexico City?
Mylo:	No, (2.) <u>I wasn't</u>. (3.) <u>I was</u> born in a small village.
Interviewer:	(4.) <u>Were you</u> interested in music as a child?
Mylo:	Yes. I started to play the guitar when (5.) <u>I was</u> eight.
Interviewer:	Wow! (6.) <u>That's</u> young! Tell me about your life now.
Mylo:	Well, (7.) <u>I'm</u> married now. My wife and I have a daughter. (8.) <u>She'll be</u> two next week.
Interviewer:	Congratulations! And what are your future plans?
Mylo:	Well, (9.) <u>I'll be</u> in Europe next month.
Interviewer:	(10.) <u>Will you be</u> in Miami again soon?
Mylo:	No, I'm sorry, (11.) <u>I won't</u>.
Interviewer:	That's too bad for us. Well, good luck on your tour!

B

	Verb Tense	Words after BE
1. My parents were <u>farmers</u>.	past	noun
2. I was <u>happy</u> to practice the guitar.	past	adjective
3. My daughter will be a <u>musician</u>.	future	noun
4. Your new song is <u>popular</u>.	present	adjective
5. You're a very famous <u>singer</u>.	present	noun
6. My wife won't be in <u>Europe</u> next month.	future	noun
7. I'll be <u>at your next concert</u>.	future	PP

Lesson 9: Student Book

A

1. (walk)   My son Mark walks home from school.   T   (F)
2. (arrive) The bus arrives at 6:00 p.m.   T   (F)
3. (cook)   I cook dinner when we get home.   (T)   F
4. (study) Mark studies when he   T   (F)
5. (get)   gets home.
6. (play)   Mark plays computer games.   (T)   F
7. (have)   My husband Charlie has coffee   T   (F)
8. (come)   when he comes home.
9. (relax) He relaxes on the couch.   (T)   F
10. (wash) I wash the dishes after we eat.   T   (F)
11. (do)   My son does his homework   (T)   F
12. (go)   before he goes to bed.

B

1. Mark doesn't walk home from school. He takes the bus.
2. The bus doesn't arrive at 6:00 p.m. It arrives at 5:00 p.m.
3. Mark doesn't study when he gets home. He plays computer games.
4. Your husband Charlie doesn't have coffee when he comes home. He has a snack.
5. You don't wash the dishes after you eat. Your husband Charlie washes the dishes.

C Possible answers:
1. Charlie looks at his mail when he gets home./When Charlie gets home, he looks at his mail./Charlie looks at his mail after he gets home./After Charlie gets home, he looks at his mail.
2. Charlie changes his clothes after he looks at his mail./After he looks at his mail, Charlie changes his clothes.
3. After he changes his clothes, Charlie has a snack.
4. After he eats dinner, Charlie washes the dishes./Charlie washes the dishes after he eats dinner.
5. Before he goes to sleep, Charlie reads./After he washes the dishes, Charlie reads.
6. After he reads, Charlie goes to sleep./Charlie goes to sleep after he reads.

Review Lessons 6–9: Student Book

A

(Mike) doesn't want to go to the doctor every year for a check-up, but (he) goes. Before (he) goes, (he) gets very nervous because (he) worries about his health. When (he) is in the doctor's office, (he) answers many questions. But (he) doesn't like the doctor's questions about exercise. (Mike) likes to sit on the couch, relax, eat junk food, and watch TV. (He)'s a couch potato.

B

Mike has a new life (1.) because he exercises every day. His doctor told him he has high blood pressure, (2.) so he wants to improve his health. Now he feels better (3.) and/because he has more energy.

(4.) When he goes to the gym, he lifts weights for a half hour (5.) or/and/before/after he uses the treadmill for the same amount of time. He takes a shower (6.) after/when he's done, and then he goes home to walk the dog. Then he eats out, (7.) or he eats at home. He doesn't eat junk food anymore, (8.) and/so/but sometimes he misses it.

(9.) Before he changed his lifestyle, he had high blood pressure (10.) and other health problems (11.) because he didn't take care of himself. Now he's a new man!

C
1. Mike was born in Vancouver.
2. He is 25 years old.
3. Mike he exercises a lot.
4. He goes to the gym a lot. He is very energetic.
5. He eats well because he wants to be healthy.
6. He will be very healthy.
7. He will Will he have normal blood pressure?
8. He won't be a couch potato anymore.
9. He isn't wasn't careful about his health in the past.
10. Whenever he gets exercise, he feels good.
11. He don't doesn't like to eat junk food now.
12. At the gym, Mike lifts weights, uses the treadmill, and takes a shower.

Have Fun Lessons 6–9: Student Book

A

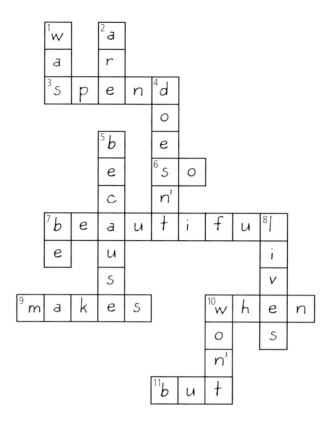

Lesson 10: Student Book

A

Lynn: Hi, Janet. What (1. <u>are you doing</u>/do you do) right now?

Janet: Well, I (2. <u>'m trying</u>/try) to write my essay, but I can't concentrate. My neighbor (3. <u>is playing</u>/plays) loud music. Can you hear it?

Lynn: Yes! That's terrible. (4. Is he always making/<u>Does he always make</u>) so much noise?

Janet: Yes. He (5. is playing/<u>plays</u>) in a band once a week. He and his friends (6. are practicing/<u>practice</u>) every night, and I'm getting tired of it. So, what (7. <u>are you doing</u>/do you do) now? Do you want to meet me at Biff's Café?

Lynn: Sure!

B

Lynn: What's going on? Biff's is so crowded! Whenever I (1.) <u>come</u> here, it's empty.

Janet: Look! That's Mylo, the famous rock star! He (2.) <u>'s playing</u> his guitar!

Lynn: You're kidding! I can't believe Mylo (3.) <u>'s performing</u> here.

Janet: He (4.) <u>gives</u> surprise free concerts when he (5.) <u>travels</u>. Listen, he (6.) <u>'s singing</u> my favorite song.

Lynn: It's hard to hear.

Janet: Some people (7.) <u>are dancing</u>.

Lynn: Really? Where? There's no place to dance.

Janet: Look! Someone (8.) <u>is coming</u> to the door.

Lynn: What's he saying?

Janet: Mylo (9.) <u>'s playing</u> tomorrow night again! He (10.) <u>'s giving</u> us free tickets!

STUDENT BOOK ANSWER KEY

Lesson 11: Student Book

A

Dear Mom,

Hi! I hope all is well. School is OK. As you know, (1. I take/**I'm taking**) three classes: English, art, and math. (2. **I like**/I'm liking) the art and English classes, but (3. I have/**I'm having**) trouble with my math class. The teacher (4. **knows**/is knowing) that the class is difficult for me. (5. **She often helps me**/She's often helping) me with my homework after class, but (6. **I still don't understand**/I'm still not understanding) it. In fact, (7. I think about/**I'm thinking about**) dropping my math class.

Mom, please understand. (8. **I have**/I'm having) a lot of homework in my other classes. (9. **I want**/I'm wanting) to get good grades at school, so (10. **I really think**/I'm really thinking) that I should drop the class. Please don't be angry!

B

BASE FORM	Form in Exercise A	Non-Action Verb	Action Verb
1. take	'm taking		✓
2. have	'm having		✓
3. know	knows	✓	
4. understand	understand	✓	
5. think about	'm thinking about	✓	✓
6. have	have	✓	
7. think that	think that	✓	

C

Jan: I got an email from Paula today. She (1.) <u>'s not doing well</u> in her math class, and she (2.) <u>wants</u> to drop it. She (3.) <u>doesn't need</u> math because she (4.) <u>'s studying art</u>. And she (5.) <u>'s taking</u> two other classes now. That's a lot with her part-time job.

Ken: Well, I (6.) <u>think</u> that math is very important. She (7.) <u>needs</u> to stay in her math class.

Jan: I'm sorry, Ken. I (8.) <u>don't agree</u> with you about this. Let's talk about it more tomorrow.

Lesson 12: Student Book

A

Last year, I decided to go to Vietnam to visit my family. I <u>made</u> my reservation and <u>bought</u> my ticket online. I <u>was</u> very excited about my trip.

The day of my trip <u>was</u> terrible. First, I almost missed the plane because the taxi <u>came</u> to my house 30 minutes late. Then I <u>had</u> to stand in line and go through security. I <u>was</u> in such a hurry that I <u>left</u> one of my bags on the floor. A nice woman <u>ran</u> after me and <u>gave</u> me my bag. Finally, I <u>found</u> the right gate. When I <u>got</u> to my seat, I <u>sat</u> down, <u>read</u> the newspaper, and <u>fell</u> asleep.

Base Form	Past Tense
make	made
buy	bought
be	was
come	came
have	had
leave	left
run	ran
give	gave
find	found
get	got
sit	sat
read	read
fall	fell

B
1. (T) F   That's true. Last year Sam went to Vietnam.
2. (T) F   That's true. He bought his ticket online.
3. T (F)   He didn't miss the plane.
4. T (F)   He didn't take the bus to the airport.
5. T (F)   He didn't leave his bag on the bus.
6. (T) F   That's true. A woman gave him his bag.

C Possible Answers:

My wife and I (1.) <u>came</u> to the United States ten years ago. At that time, the economic situation in my country was very bad. I (2.) <u>didn't have</u> a good job.

When we (3.) <u>arrived/got/came</u> here, our life was very difficult. We (4.) <u>didn't speak/know</u> much English. I (5.) <u>got/had</u> a job as a carpenter, and my wife (6.) <u>took</u> an English course. After a while, we (7.) <u>saved</u> money and (8.) <u>moved</u> to California.

Lesson 13: Student Book

A

Sylvia: I need to get some cash. Let's stop at the ATM. You know, Bob, when I was young, we didn't have ATMs. We (1.) <u>used to wait in line</u> at the bank to withdraw money.
Bob: Really?
Sylvia: Yes. I remember that I (2.) <u>used to go</u> to the bank during my lunch hour. Sometimes I didn't have time for lunch!
Bob: So, do you think things are easier now, Grandma?
Sylvia: Well, I think in many ways, life (3.) <u>used to be</u> easier. For example, when I was a child, we never (4.) <u>used to buy</u> milk in the grocery store. The milkman (5.) <u>used to deliver</u> milk to our house. And when we were sick, the doctor (6.) <u>used to come</u> to our house, too. We didn't have to drive to the doctor's office.
Bob: Wow! Did you (7.) <u>used to ride</u> a horse to school, too?
Sylvia: Come on, Bob! I'm not *that* old!

B

1. In the 1950s, gas used to cost only 25 cents a gallon.
2. In the 1960s, many men used to have long hair in the United States.
3. A long time ago, people used to think that the world was flat.
4. Did people used to think that men lived on Mars?
5. More people used to smoke cigarettes 50 years ago.
6. Doctors used to make house calls many years ago, but now people have to go to the doctor.
7. Women didn't used to wear pants before the 1920s.
8. Did women in the U.S. used to have the right to vote in the 1800s?
9. People used to have a lot of children to help them do the work on farms.
10. A long time ago, people never used to cook with artificial ingredients.

C

When I was a child, I had an easy life. I never <u>used to work</u> very hard. I <u>used to walk</u> a short distance to school every morning. After school, my friends and I <u>used to stop</u> at the candy store on the way home. Then we <u>used to play</u> games outside until it got dark. My mother <u>used to</u> just <u>shout</u> my name when it was time for dinner. Yes, my life <u>used to be</u> very easy.

Review Lessons 10–13: Student Book

A

I used to dream about being on TV, and last year I(got)free tickets to a TV show in Hollywood. I(took)my best friend with me, and we arrived early to get good seats. But we(didn't)get in right away. We(stood)in line for about an hour, and then we finally(went)in. After a while, the director talked to the audience and showed us the "applause" signs. I(thought)that was funny. After that, the star of the show(came)out and joked with us. Then we(had)to be very quiet, and the show started. When the applause signs(went)on, we(made)a lot of noise. The show(wasn't)very interesting, but we(had)a good experience.

B

Every year, I get free tickets to a TV show in Hollywood. I take my best friend with me, and we arrive early to get good seats. But we don't get in right away. We stand in line for about an hour, and then we finally go in. After a while, the director talks to the audience and shows us the "applause" signs. I think that is funny. After that, the star of the show comes out and jokes with us. Then we have to be very quiet, and the show starts. When the applause signs go on, we make a lot of noise. The show isn't very interesting, but we have a good experience.

C

Steven: What (1.) <u>are you looking</u> at?
Jennifer: The tickets for the TV show.
Steven: When (2.) <u>are we going</u>?
Jennifer: Steven, (3.) <u>I know</u> (4.) <u>you want</u> to go, but this year (5.) <u>I feel</u> like staying home. (6.) <u>I don't want</u> to go.
Steven: (7.) <u>I don't believe</u> it! What (8.) <u>are you saying</u>? (9.) <u>We go</u> every year.
Jennifer: (10.) <u>I don't have to</u> go. (11.) <u>I know</u> the tickets were free, but it's a pain to go in all that L.A. traffic.
Steven: You surprise me. Listen, (12.) <u>I think</u> that I can change your mind. Will you go if I drive this time?

D

1. ~~Always~~ Jennifer <u>always</u> gets free tickets.
2. She visits ~~once a year~~ Los Angeles <u>once a year</u>.
3. She didn't want~~ed~~ to drive.
4. When she goes, she <u>has</u> ~~is having~~ a good time.
5. Jennifer and her friend <u>are</u> sitting in good seats right now.
6. They are <u>laughing</u> ~~laugh~~ and <u>talking</u> ~~talk~~ a lot.
7. She <u>likes</u> ~~is liking~~ to do this because it's free and fun.
8. Two years ago, her best friend didn't <u>go</u> ~~went~~ with her because she had a cold.
9. Did she <u>buy</u> ~~bought~~ the tickets?
10. They wanted to <u>see</u> ~~saw~~ famous people in Hollywood.
11. Jennifer's friend used to <u>think</u> ~~thinking~~ about a career in acting.
12. ~~Was~~ <u>Did</u> she go to Hollywood?

Have Fun Lessons 10–13: Student Book

A

understood
thought
knew
brought
rode
wrote
enjoyed
bought
slept
caught
taught
paid
put
stayed
spoke
swam
threw

Secret Message: Don't worry. Be happy!

Lesson 14: Student Book

A

Anne: Your brother called this morning. (1.) <u>Are you going to call</u> him back?
Charlie: No, (2.) <u>I'm not going to call</u> him. I'm too busy.
Anne: But it's his birthday tomorrow.
Charlie: Oh, you're right!
Anne: (3.) <u>Are you going to buy</u> him a present?
Charlie: Maybe. I think (4.) <u>I'm going to get</u> him a fishing rod. (5.) <u>He and Nancy are going to retire</u> soon, and I know they both enjoy fishing.
Anne: That's true. You know, we should invite them over for dinner Saturday.
Charlie: Good idea!
Anne: Wait! I forgot. (6.) <u>We're not going to be</u> home.
Charlie: Why not?
Anne: Remember? It's our anniversary. (7.) <u>You're going to take</u> me out to dinner!

B
1. I will call him back.
2. Are you going to call him back?
3. We probably won't be home.
4. He's not going to call him back today.
5. Will they call him today?
6. She's going to call back later.

C
1. Q: <u>Is Charlie going to call his brother now?</u>
   A: No, Charlie isn't going to call his brother now.
2. Q: <u>Will his brother be at their anniversary dinner?/Is his brother going to be at their anniversary dinner?</u>
   A: No, his brother won't be at their anniversary dinner.
3. Q: What will Charlie probably get his brother for his birthday?
   A: <u>He/Charlie will probably get his brother a fishing rod for his birthday.</u>

D Possible answers:
Anne is going to go to her computer class the day after tomorrow.
Anne is going to celebrate her anniversary on February 6.
She is going to go to a Valentine's party next weekend.
She is going to pick up Jasmine at the airport next Monday.
She is going to get a haircut on February 10.
She will probably buy Valentine's cards on February 11.
She will probably take a trip to Atlanta on February 13.

Various answers are possible for the negative sentences.

Lesson 15: Student Book

A

Theresa
- _c_ 1. Please come to the wedding.
- _e_ 2. They're getting married, and they're only twenty.
- _a_ 3. I have so much to do.
- _d_ 4. We're going to meet his parents tomorrow for lunch.
- _b_ 5. Please don't tell them that I'm worried.
- _f_ 6. There are so many invitations to write.

Elizabeth
a. I'll help you. Call any time.
b. Don't worry. I won't.
c. I promise. I'll be there.
d. I hope you'll like each other.
e. They love each other very much. I'm sure they'll be happy.
f. I'll write them for you.

Elizabeth
- _i_ 7. Are you planning to order flowers?
- _k_ 8. Let me do the invitations for you!
- _j_ 9. Are they going to go on a honeymoon?
- _h_ 10. I don't have a car
- _g_ 11. Be happy for them! Try to relax!

Theresa
g. OK, I'll try.
h. I'll find someone to give you a ride.
i. Yes, I think I'll buy roses.
j. No, they probably won't. They don't have much money.
k. No, I won't let you! It's too much work.

B

Theresa: Emily, (1.) <u>I hope you'll stay</u> in school.
Emily: Don't worry, Mom. (2.) <u>I'll stay</u> in school. I promise! I want to be a teacher. You know that.
Theresa: I know. I just wanted to hear you say it. (3.) <u>I'm sure you'll be</u> a great teacher.
Emily: Well, thanks Mom. (4.) <u>I hope you'll relax</u>. You worry too much.
Theresa: But that's what mothers do, honey! Anyway, I have to get off the phone right now to work on the invitations.
Emily: Mom, please let me do the invitations. It's my wedding.
Theresa: No, (5.) <u>I won't</u>. I don't mind doing them.
Emily: (6.) OK. But <u>I'll help</u> you.

Lesson 16: Student Book

A

Tom: Are you ready for your job interview?
Alice: I'm so worried about it! <u>If I don't get this job</u>, I'm going to be so disappointed.
Tom: But you're so talented. The interviewer will be very impressed with you <u>when he meets you</u>.
Alice: But I'm so nervous. I don't know what I'm going to say <u>if he asks me about my job experience</u>. I don't have any job experience!
Tom: You're only 16 years old. <u>If he expects a lot of experience</u>, I'll be surprised.
Alice: I guess you're right. I'm going to eat something <u>before I go to the interview</u>.
Tom: OK. <u>After you eat</u>, I'll help you prepare.

B

Time/If Clause	Comma?	Main Clause
1. If I don't get this job,	✓	I'm going to be so disappointed!
2. If he expects a lot of job experience,	✓	I'll be surprised.
3. After you eat,	✓	I'll help you prepare.

Main Clause		*Time/If* Clause
4. The interviewer will be very impressed with you	___	when he meets you.
5. I don't know what I'm going to say	___	if he asks me about my job experience.
6. I'm going to eat something	___	before I go to the interview.

C

My job interview is in three hours. Before I (1.) <u>leave</u>, I (2.) <u>'m going to practice</u> for the interview with my brother. I (3.) <u>will try</u> to relax when I (4.) <u>get</u> to the office. If the interviewer (5.) <u>asks</u> me about my job experience, I (6.) <u>will tell</u> the truth. My brother (7.) <u>is going to take</u> me out when the interview (8.) <u>is</u> over. What will I do if the interviewer (9.) <u>doesn't like</u> me?

Lesson 17: Student Book

A
1. Steve is getting married this afternoon. T **F**
2. The ceremony begins at 1:00 p.m. T **F**
3. Steve isn't going to college right away. **T** F
4. Mrs. Cho is having a party for Steve. **T** F
5. Mr. Parker and his wife are coming to the party. T **F**
6. The store closes at 5:00 p.m. **T** F
7. Mr. Parker isn't coming by tomorrow. **T** F
8. The Parkers' flight leaves tomorrow night. T **F**

B Possible Answers:
1. When is Steve graduating? He's graduating today.
2. What time does graduation begin? It begins at 2:00 this afternoon.
3. Is Steve going to college right away? No. He's not going to college right away. He's going in a year or two.
4. Are Mr. Parker and his wife coming to the party? No, they're not. Mr. Parker has to work in his shop.
5. What time does the store close? It closes at 5:00.
6. What time does the Parkers' flight leave? It leaves at 7:00 tomorrow morning.
7. How are they getting to the airport? They're taking a cab.

Review Lessons 14–17: Student Book

A

Art and I leave at 6:00 tomorrow morning for Seattle. Before we leave, I'm going to drink a cup of strong coffee. We're driving separately. If we get there by lunchtime, I'll be happy. When we get there, we're going to unload the truck and Art will return it right away. I'll follow him to the truck rental place, and then we'll take a break and have lunch. If we don't rest for a little while, we'll be exhausted. After we have lunch, we'll start unpacking. I hope we'll be OK. Moving is so much work!

B Possible answers:

Claire and I are moving to Seattle tomorrow. She's worried, but I'm not. If we (1.) get there at midnight, that (2.) will be OK with me. Before we (3.) leave, I (4.) 'm going to have/eat a big breakfast and (5.) read the newspaper. After I (6.) have/eat breakfast, I (7.) 'll get gas for the truck. During the trip, if I (8.) am/get hungry or tired, I (9.) 'll take a break. When we (10.) get to our new house, Claire (11.) will want me to unload the truck right away. But I have another idea. I think I'll take a nap first.

D

PLANS THAT ARE CERTAIN	PLANS THAT ARE NOT CERTAIN
I'm not going to go out today.	I probably won't go out today.
I'm going to stay home and relax.	I'll probably stay home and relax.
They're going to go to the movies.	They'll probably go to the movies.
We aren't going to be home tomorrow.	We probably won't be home tomorrow.
He's going to cook dinner.	He'll probably cook dinner.

E Possible Answers:
1. I'll drive you.
2. I promise that I'll tell you the truth.
3. Don't worry. I won't.
4. I'll help you.
5. No. I won't let you drive without a license.
6. I hope that they have a good time.
7. You'll do fine.

Have Fun Lessons 14–17: Student Book

A

Student A Questions and Answers
1. What are they doing this afternoon?   Visiting Alex.
2. What are they doing tonight?   Going to the theater.
3. What time does the show start?   7 p.m.
4. What are they going to do on the 21st?   Probably go away for the weekend.
5. What are they going to do on Suzanne's birthday?   Go to a party at Nancy's.
6. When does Suzanne's Spanish class start?   On the 10th.

Student B Questions and Answers
1. What are they going to do on their anniversary?   Probably have dinner out.
2. What is Larry going to do on April 16th?   Go to Portland.
3. What time does his flight leave?   9:00 a.m.
4. What time does he get to Portland?   11:15 a.m.
5. What are they going to do on April 14th?   Mail their taxes.

Lesson 18: Student Book

A

Marta: <u>Did</u> you come to this country by yourself?
Anya: No, I came here with some other students.
Miles: <u>Were</u> you born in a small town?
Anya: No, I wasn't. I was born in a big city.
Tom: <u>Are</u> you having a good time at this school?
Anya: Yes, I'm having a wonderful time.
Marta: <u>Do</u> you think American boys are cute?
Anya: Of course I do!
Miles: <u>Are</u> you ready to go back to your country?
Anya: Not at all!
Tom: <u>Does</u> your family miss you?
Anya: Of course! I miss my family, too!
Marta: <u>Are</u> you leaving soon?
Anya: Uh-huh. I'm leaving in about four weeks.
Miles: <u>Will</u> you come back to visit us?
Anya: I hope so!

B Possible Answers:
1. Kim: <u>Did you interview Anya today?</u>
   Marta: Yes, I did interview Anya. She was very interesting.
2. Kim: <u>Is she leaving soon?</u>
   Marta: Yes, she's leaving the United States in four weeks.
3. Kim: <u>Does she like American food?</u>
   Marta: Yes, she loves American food, especially hot dogs.
4. Kim: <u>Did she talk about her family?</u>
   Marta: Yes, she talked about her family.
5. Kim: <u>Does she have any brothers and sisters?</u>
   Marta: Yes, she has two brothers and two sisters.
6. Kim: <u>Do her parents live in a big city?</u>
   Marta: No, her parents live in a small town.
7. Kim: <u>Are her parents coming to the United States?</u>
   Marta: No, her parents aren't coming to the United States.
8. Kim: <u>Is she ready to go back to her country?</u>
   Marta: No, she isn't ready to go back to her country.
9. Kim: <u>Is the school going to have a party for her?</u>
   Marta: Yes, the school is going to have a big party for her next week.
10. Kim: <u>Will she come back for a visit?</u>
    Marta: I don't know. I hope she'll come back and visit us some day.

Lesson 19: Student Book

A
1. Where was he born?
   a. In Asia.   (b.) In Europe.
2. When did he come to the United States?
   (a.) When he was a child.   b. When he was 25.
3. How did his family get to this country?
   (a.) By boat.   b. By plane.
4. How was the trip?
   a. Wonderful.   (b.) Terrible.
5. Where does he live now?
   a. In New York.   (b.) In Florida.
6. What do his friends do at the clubhouse?
   (a.) Play cards.   b. Eat lunch.
7. When will Pam be in Florida?
   (a.) Next week.   b. Next year.
8. Why is she going to Florida?
   (a.) Her boss is sending her.   b. For a vacation.

B
1. Q: When did Karen come to the U.S.?
   A: Two years ago.
2. Q: Why was she lonely?
   A: Because she was the only person in her class from Taiwan.
3. Q: Where did she fall down?
   A: On the sidewalk.
4. Q: What did she break?
   A: Her leg.
5. Q: Who called an ambulance?
   A: A very kind man.
6. Q: How is her English now?
   A: Excellent.
7. Q: When are they going to have a baby?
   A: Next year.

Lesson 20: Student Book

A

Mom: How are you doing?
John: I'm (1.) <u>doing</u> fine.
Mom: How's your roommate Paul?
John: He's OK, but he's not a very neat person. He (2.) <u>doesn't do</u> anything around the house.
Mom: What do you mean?
John: Well he likes to cook, but after he eats, he never (3.) <u>does</u> the dishes. And he never (4.) <u>does</u> his laundry. His dirty clothes are in a big pile next to his bed.
Mom: Oh, my! (5.) <u>Do</u> you tell him to clean up?
John: Yes, I asked him to wash the dishes last night, but he (6.) <u>didn't do</u> them. He just left the dishes in the sink.
Mom: That's terrible. (7.) <u>Do</u> you wash your dishes, John?
John: Of course, Mom. I always clean up!
Mom: Well, tell Paul that he has to do something around the house. Tell him if he (8.) <u>doesn't do</u> any chores, you'll look for a new roommate. By the way, how's school? (9.) <u>Do</u> you have a lot of homework?
John: Yes. In fact, I'm (10.) <u>doing</u> my homework right now.

B

	HV	MV		HV	MV
1. doing	___	✓	6. didn't do	✓	✓
2. doesn't do	✓	✓	7. do	✓	___
3. does	___	✓	8. doesn't do	✓	✓
4. does	___	✓	9. do	✓	___
5. do	✓	___	10. doing	___	✓

C

	Affirmative	Negative	Yes-No Question
Singular/ Present	John does his homework every day.	John doesn't do his homework every day.	Does John do his homework every day?
Plural/ Present	They do their homework every day.	They don't do their homework every day.	Do they do their homework every day?
Singular/ Past	He did his homework yesterday.	He didn't do his homework yesterday.	Did he do his homework yesterday?
Plural/ Past	They did their homework yesterday.	They didn't do their homework yesterday.	Did they do their homework yesterday?

Review Lessons 18–20: Student Book

A

Reporter: Ms. Bates, what are your plans to improve our schools?
Ms. Bates: I'm going to do a lot. I will do my best to give our children everything they need.
Reporter: What did you do for education when you were a mayor?
Ms. Bates: I did a lot of work. I started programs for parents. I did my best to help our kids learn.
Reporter: Did you help teachers?
Ms. Bates: I sure did.
Reporter: Were you successful?
Ms. Bates: Yes, in some ways. But I will do more when I'm governor.
Reporter: Where are you going to get the money?
Ms. Bates: Don't worry. I'll find it.
Reporter: Were you careful with money when you were a mayor?
Ms. Bates: I sure was! Why are you asking me that question? I did a great job as mayor!

B

Past Tense	Present Tense	Present Continuous Tense	Future Tense (will or be going to)
Where was the party?	Where is the party?	-----------------	Where will the party be?/ Where is the party going to be?
When did the movie start?	When does the movie start?	When is the movie starting?	When will the movie start?/ When is the movie going to start?
Why did they do the shopping?	Why do they do the shopping?	Why are they doing the shopping?	Why are they going to do the shopping?/ Why will they do the shopping?

C

Questions with DO

1. Where do you usually do your homework?
2. What time did you do your homework last night?
3. Do you do the laundry in your house?
4. Did you do a good job on our last test?

D

1. They ~~will~~ are going to do the laundry later.
2. Were ~~Y~~you born in this country?
3. Where ~~you~~ were you born?
4. Who are you visiting?
5. Why did you do ~~did~~ your homework in the kitchen?
6. Where ~~are~~ do you live?
7. When did he ~~came~~ come home?
8. She ~~don't~~ doesn't do her best.
9. Did you ~~did~~ do your homework on time?
10. I will ~~doing~~ do my laundry in a few minutes.
11. ~~You will~~ Will you leave tomorrow?
12. Where ~~are~~ do they come from?/Where are they ~~come~~ from?
13. Can you ~~make~~ do me a favor?
14. Yesterday I relaxed and ~~do~~ did nothing.
15. I am ~~do~~ doing a good job on this exercise.
16. ~~We are~~ Are we doing our best today?

Have Fun Lessons 18–20: Student Book

Various answers are possible.

Lesson 21: Student Book

A

c 1. Who(S) went(V) to a party?
h 2. Who did(V) Nina(S) go(V) to the party with?
f 3. Who(S) drove(V) her home?
b 4. Who's(S,V) getting(V) married?
a 5. Who is(V) she(S) going to marry(V)?
g 6. Who(S) will(V) be(V) very happy?
e 7. Who did(V) Nina(S) meet(V) at the party?
d 8. Who(S) has(V) Nina's cell phone?

a. A guy she works with.
b. Jan is.
c. Nina did.
d. Her brother.
e. A nice guy.
f. Cindy.
g. Jan will.
h. Lots of kids from school.

B

1. Who(S) is(V) going to marry(V) Jan?
2. Who is(V) Jan(S) going to marry(V)?
3. Who(S) will(V) be(V) happy?
4. Who did(V) Nina(S) go(V) to the party with?
5. Who(S) drove(V) Nina home?
6. Who did(V) Nina(S) meet(V) at the party?
7. Who(S) is(V) in love with Jan?
8. Who is(V) Jan(S) in love with?
9. Who does(V) Nina(S) talk(V) to about her life?

C

1. Who is/Who's a busy student?
2. Who has children?
3. Who was home last night?
4. Who went to a party last night?
5. Who's tired today?
6. Who's learning a lot of English?
7. Who wants to go home after class?
8. Who likes to dance?

Lesson 22: Student Book

A

Conversation 1

1. <u>How does</u> Julie get to school?
   a. She takes the bus.   (b.) She drives.
2. <u>How far does</u> she live from here?
   a. She lives a few blocks from here.   (b.) She lives far away from school.
3. <u>How long does</u> it take her to get here by car?
   (a.) It depends on the traffic.   b. Only a few minutes.
4. <u>How often does</u> she go to school?
   a. Every day.   (b.) Three times a week.

Conversation 2

1. <u>How far is</u> the museum from here?
   (a.) About two miles from here.   b. About ten miles from here.
2. <u>How often does</u> the bus come?
   a. It comes once a day.   (b.) It comes every five minutes.
3. <u>How long does</u> it take to get there by bus?
   a. It takes about an hour.   (b.) It takes about ten minutes.

B

Ted: Where are you from, Kyung?
Kyung: I'm from Pusan. It's a city in Korea.
Ted: I've never heard of Pusan. (1.) <u>How far is Pusan from Seoul?</u>
Kyung: About 500 miles. It's a beautiful city.
Ted: I'd like to go there some day. (2.) <u>How often do you go back there/to Korea?</u>
Kyung: Oh, I usually go back to Korea once a year. It's such a long trip!
Ted: (3.) <u>How long does it take to get there?</u>
Kyung: It takes about fifteen hours by plane.
Ted: That *is* a very long trip. So tell me, do you live in a dorm?
Kyung: No, I live with my relatives in Mason.
Ted: Mason? I don't know where that is. (4.) <u>How far is it from here?</u>
Kyung: I think it's about 50 miles from here.
Ted: (5.) <u>How do you get here?</u>
Kyung: My uncle gives me a ride. He works here.
Ted: That's lucky. So, (6.) <u>how are your classes?</u>
Kyung: My classes are wonderful. I'm learning a lot.

C

1. How often do you come to school?
2. How do you get to school?
3. How far is this school from your house?
4. How long does it usually take you to get to school?

Lesson 23: Student Book

A

Nick: Laura! It's time to go to school. (1.) <u>Aren't</u> you getting up? (2.) <u>Doesn't</u> school start at 8:30?
Laura: I don't have to get up early. I'm not going to school today.
Nick: Why (3.) <u>aren't</u> you going?
Laura: (4.) <u>Didn't</u> I tell you? We don't have school today.
Nick: Oh right, I forgot! So, what are you going to do?
Laura: I'm going to the movies with my friend Sam.
Nick: But (5.) <u>don't</u> you have homework to do?
Laura: Yes, we both have homework, but we can do it when we get home.
Nick: Why (6.) <u>don't</u> you stay home and do your homework together?
Laura: Don't worry, Dad. We don't have much. We can do it tonight.

B

1. Aren't you tired?
2. Aren't you hungry?
3. Didn't you go to the movies?
4. Why didn't you call me?
5. Weren't you home?
6. Why don't we go out for dinner?
7. Why don't you stay home and do your homework?

Lesson 24: Student Book

A

1. The Olympic games began in Greece more than 2,000 years ago, but the modern Olympics <u>didn't</u> begin until 1898.
2. Many countries <u>didn't</u> send athletes to the first modern Olympics.
3. There <u>weren't</u> many sports at the first modern Olympics, but today, there are hundreds of sports.
4. Not every sport is played in the Olympics. For example, windsurfing is an Olympic sport, but skateboarding and golf <u>aren't</u>.
5. A long time ago, women <u>didn't</u> participate in the Olympics.
6. Some countries still <u>don't</u> send women athletes to the Olympics.
7. Now soccer is popular in the U.S., but it <u>wasn't</u> popular 30 years ago.
8. The U.S. has many good Olympic teams, but it <u>doesn't</u> always have the best teams.
9. The 2012 Olympics <u>won't</u> be in New York. They might be in Paris.
10. Some people think that Olympic medal winners <u>shouldn't</u> be able to make a lot of money in advertisements.

B

Karina: I think baseball will be the number one sport in France.
Jean: I disagree. Baseball (1. be) <u>won't be</u> the number one sport. Soccer will be the most popular sport there for years to come.
Karina: I think American football and soccer are the same.
Jean: No, American football and soccer (2. be) <u>aren't</u> the same. In fact, they're completely different.
Karina: Can soccer players throw the ball?
Jean: Well, the goalie can throw the ball, but the other soccer players (3. touch) <u>can't touch</u> the ball with their hands.
Karina: That's interesting. I think Pele is a soccer player from Argentina. Am I right?
Jean: Well, Pele is a soccer player, but he (4. be) <u>isn't</u> from Argentina. He's from Brazil.
Karina: I think the United States won the World Cup last year.
Jean: No. The United States (5. win) <u>didn't win</u> the World Cup last year. You know, you (6. know) <u>don't know</u> much about sports, Karina!
Karina: But I'm trying to learn. You (7. laugh) <u>shouldn't laugh</u> at me!

C

1. Were you a good athlete when you were a child?
   X wasn't a good athlete when he/she was a child.
2. Did you play baseball or soccer when you were a child?
   X didn't play baseball or soccer when he/she was a child.
3. Could you swim fast when you were a child?
   X couldn't swim fast when he/she was a child.
4. Do you love sports?
   X doesn't love sports.
5. Are you a good athlete?
   X isn't a good athlete.
6. Are you taking an exercise class now?
   X isn't taking an exercise class now.
7. Do you think you should watch sports on TV every Saturday?
   X doesn't think he/she should watch sports on TV every Saturday.

Review Lessons 21–24: Student Book

A

Brad Jr.: Dad, can I take the car to Adam's house?
Brad Sr.: Who's Adam?
Brad Jr.: He's a kid in my class.
Brad Sr.: Oh, right. Weren't you at his house last Saturday?
Brad Jr.: Uh-huh.
Brad Sr.: Who else is going to be there?
Brad Jr.: I don't know. Probably his parents.
Brad Sr.: Oh, don't I know them? Aren't they doctors?
Brad Jr.: I don't think so. I think they're lawyers.
Brad Sr.: Well, how far is Adam's house from here?
Brad Jr.: About ten minutes, I think.
Brad Sr.: How long will you be there?
Brad Jr.: I'm not sure. Maybe a couple of hours.
Brad Sr.: Don't you have to clean your room?
Brad Jr.: It isn't dirty.
Brad Sr.: Can't you ride your bike?
Brad Jr.: No, I can't. I have a flat tire.
Brad Sr.: Well, why don't we fix it?
Brad Jr.: Dad, *please* let me drive!

B

1. Who did Brad Jr. want to visit?
2. Who's going to be at Adam's house?
3. Who else will be there?
4. Why can't Brad ride his bike?
5. Why didn't he ride his bike?
6. Why isn't he cleaning his room?
7. How long does it take to get to Adam's house?
8. How often do the two boys visit?
9. Doesn't Brad have a driver license?
10. Isn't Brad a good driver?

C

Present *don't/doesn't* or *isn't/aren't*		Present Continuous	Future with *Won't*	*Can't*
1. Brad Sr. doesn't eat fast food.	X	Brad Sr. isn't eating fast food.	Brad Sr. won't eat fast food.	Brad Sr. can't eat fast food.
2. Brad Jr. doesn't drive fast.	X	Brad Jr. isn't driving fast.	Brad Jr. won't drive fast.	Brad Jr. can't drive fast.
3. X	Brad Jr. isn't late.	X	Brad Jr. won't be late.	Brad Jr. can't be late.
4. Brad Jr. doesn't ride his bike.	X	Brad Jr. isn't riding his bike.	Brad Jr. won't ride his bike.	Brad Jr. can't ride his bike.
5. X	They aren't home.	X	They won't be home.	They can't be home.
6. They don't stay out late.	X	They aren't staying out late.	They won't stay out late.	They can't stay out late.

Have Fun Lessons 21–24

Various answers are possible.

Lesson 25: Student Book

A

Mom: What a mess! Please help us clean up, Mollie.
Mollie: OK, Mom. (1.) <u>Whose</u> umbrella is this?
Dad: That's (2.) <u>ours</u>. Just put it in the closet.
Mollie: OK. And what about this hat?
Mom: Oh. That's (3.) <u>my sister's</u> hat. I'll take it to (4.) <u>her</u> house tomorrow.
Mollie: And how about these gloves?
Dad: I think they're (5.) <u>Grandma's</u> gloves.
Mom: Let me see them. No, they're not (6.) <u>hers</u>. They're (7.) <u>men's</u> gloves. In fact, they're (8.) <u>yours</u>!
Dad: Are you sure they're (9.) <u>mine</u>? I've never seen them before.
Mom: I'm positive. I bought them for you last year.
Dad: How did they end up in the living room?

B

	Possessive Adjective	Possessive Pronoun	Possessive Noun
1. whose	___	___	___
2. ours	___	✓	___
3. my sister's	___	___	✓
4. her	✓	___	___
5. Grandma's	___	___	✓
6. hers	___	✓	___
7. men's	___	___	✓
8. yours	___	✓	___
9. mine	___	✓	___

C

Hi, Lynn. This is your sister [C / sister's] friend, Sandy. Thank you for inviting us to you're [your] housewarming party. We enjoyed meeting you and all yours [your] friends. I'm sorry to bother you, but I think you have my jacket and I have your's [yours]! Ours [Our] jackets look very similar. Mine [C] is beige, and it looks exactly like yours [your] jacket. I'm so sorry. And I think my husband [C / husband's] jacket is also at your [C] house. His' [His] is dark brown. Can you call me? My number is 555-1114. Thanks a lot. Bye.

Lesson 26: Student Book

A

Sonia: Hey, Marta, I love your earrings. Where did you get (1.) them?
Marta: My boyfriend bought (2.) them for (3.) me. I wear (4.) them every day.
Sonia: I didn't know that you had a new boyfriend!
Marta: Well, I do. His name is Victor. I met (5.) him two months ago.
Sonia: Well, the earrings look great on (6.) you. Victor has good taste.
Marta: Thanks. I agree. Let me see your purse. Wow! Is it new?
Sonia: Uh huh. I bought (7.) it on sale at the mall last week. I love (8.) it.
Marta: It's really beautiful. So, what are you doing these days?
Sonia: Well, my brother and I are taking a grammar class at the college. Grammar isn't easy for (9.) us.
Marta: Is the class fun?
Sonia: It's difficult, but we're enjoying (10.) it very much.

B

	Object after Verb	Object after Preposition	Object Pronoun after Verb	Object Pronoun after Preposition
1. I love your earrings.	✓			
2. He bought them for me.				✓
3. I found the purse at the mall.	✓			
4. I'm taking classes with my brother.		✓		
5. We're enjoying them very much.			✓	
6. My brother is good at grammar.		✓		
7. He does very well in it.				✓

C
1. Does Marta like Sonia's earrings?
   Yes, she likes them very much.
2. How did Sonia get the earrings?
   Her boyfriend gave them to her.
3. When did Sonia meet Victor?
   She met him two months ago.
4. When did Marta buy the purse?
   She bought it last week.
5. Where are Sonia and her brother taking their grammar class?
   They're taking it at the college.
6. Is grammar easy for Sonia and her brother?
   No, it isn't easy for them.
7. Are they enjoying the grammar class?
   Yes, they're enjoying it very much.

Lesson 27: Student Book

A
Dear Annie,
   My sister has three children. They are not bad kids, but they don't behave themselves. They come to our house every Thanksgiving. They run all over the house and they never say, "please" or "thank you." They help themselves to food without asking anyone first. Last year, the oldest boy fell down and hurt himself because he was running around so much. Each year I tell myself to relax and ignore their bad behavior, but it's hard to do. My husband and I never enjoy ourselves when they visit us.
   Thanksgiving is coming. My husband said, "I want to enjoy myself this year. Let's take a trip on Thanksgiving."
   What should I do? Is my husband right? Should we take a trip? Or should we stay here and invite my sister's family to dinner?
                                    Nervous about Thanksgiving

B
1. Dear Nervous,
   Do you always say, "Make (1.) yourselves at home!" when they come to your house? I bet their house is a mess. So, when they make (2.) themselves at home at your house, they make a mess! I think your husband is right. Give (3.) yourself/yourselves a break. Take a vacation! Enjoy (4.) yourself/yourselves. Don't invite your sister for Thanksgiving this year.

2. Dear Nervous,
   I think your husband is wrong. Invite your sister and her children. They are getting older. Maybe they will behave (1.) themselves this year. Tell your husband to buy (2.) himself some earplugs. Or maybe your husband should go on vacation by (3.) himself!

3. Dear Nervous,
   Tell your sister the truth. Tell her that you and your husband can't enjoy (1.) yourselves when her children are running around the house. Your sister needs to tell her children to be more mature. You are their aunt, and you don't want them to hurt (2.) themselves at your house. If you tell the truth, you won't be upset with (3.) yourself anymore. And your sister will thank you for being honest with her.

Lesson 28: Student Book

A

Linda: Did you like the restaurant?
Bob: Yes, I did. (1. Everything/Anything) was delicious. But I'm a little disappointed. (2. Everyone/Someone/No one) called me today to say, "Happy Birthday."
Linda: You're right. I'm sorry, Bob. Hey, look! We're passing Uncle Dan's house. Let's stop and say, "Hello."
Bob: I don't think (3. anyone/no one) is home. Hello! Is anyone there? I hear (4. something/anything). I think (5. anyone/someone) is coming.
Uncle Dan: Hi, Bob! Hi, Linda. I'm sorry it took me so long to answer the door.
Bob: Uncle Dan, why is it so dark in here? Is (6. anything/nothing) wrong?
Uncle Dan: No, (7. anything/nothing) is wrong. Come on in.
Bob's friends: Surprise! Happy birthday, Bob!
Bob: Wow! (8. Everyone/No one) is here!

B

Linda: Were you surprised about the party?
Bob: I sure was! I didn't see (1.) anybody when I got to the house. (2.) Everyone/Everybody (was/were) very quiet.
Linda: I'm glad you were surprised. Do you want (3.) anything to drink?
Bob: Thanks, but not right now. I'm going to talk to Uncle Dan. He's standing over there by himself. (4.) No one/Nobody (is/are) talking to him. He doesn't know (5.) anyone/anybody here.
Bob: Thanks for planning this party, Uncle Dan.
Uncle Dan: It was my pleasure, Bob. I really didn't do (6.) anything. Your friends did all the work. You have wonderful friends. (7.) Everyone/Everybody (love/loves) you very much.

C

1. Is anyone tired?
2. Is anybody hungry?
3. Did anyone have a birthday last month?
4. Is anybody going to go home right after this class?
5. Does anyone want to get a snack after this class?

Review Lessons 25–28: Student Book

A

Nobody understands how I feel. My mother-in-law thinks my kitchen is her kitchen. But it's mine, and not hers! When she comes over, she makes herself at home. Then she tells me she wants to cook with me. But I want to cook by myself! I know she thinks I can't cook anything well. Everyone else, especially my husband, likes my cooking. I think she still wants to take care of her son.

B

My mother thinks (1.) our kitchen is her kitchen. But it's (2.) ours, not hers! When she comes over, she makes herself at home. Then she tells (3.) us she wants to cook. But we want to do it (4.) ourselves! We know she thinks that (5.) we can't cook anything. Everyone else likes (6.) our cooking.

C

(1.) My daughter-in-law doesn't want (2.) me to do anything in her kitchen. She says it's hers, not (3.) mine. She always wants to take care of everything by herself, so (4.) I never enjoy (5.) myself when I visit. Sometimes (6.) I ask (7.) myself why my wonderful son married her!

D

1. His mother's house is beautiful.
2. His parents' house is beautiful.
3. That woman's husband is a great cook.
4. Those women's husbands are great cooks.
5. The children's toys are all over the house.
6. The child's shoes are under the bed.
7. Diana's friends visited her.
8. That girl's mother is late.
9. The baby's bottle fell off the table.
10. The babies' toys are expensive.

E

AFFIRMATIVE Verb + *nothing*	NEGATIVE Verb + *not* + *anything*	YES-NO QUESTION with *anything*
He knows nothing about that.	He doesn't know anything about that.	Does he know anything about that?
He knew nothing about that.	He didn't know anything about that.	Did he know anything about that?
They did nothing about that.	They didn't do anything about that.	Did they do anything about that?
You know nothing about that.	You don't know anything about that.	Do you know anything about that?
I can do nothing about that.	I can't do anything about that.	Can I do anything about that?
She'll probably do nothing about that.	She probably won't do anything about that.	Will she do anything about that?

There + (not) BE + anyone/anybody	*There + BE + no one/nobody*	QUESTION with *anyone/anybody*
There wasn't anybody home.	There was nobody home.	Was anyone home?
There wasn't anybody there.	There was nobody there.	Was anybody there?
There isn't anyone in the kitchen.	There is nobody in the kitchen.	Is anyone in the kitchen?

Have Fun Lessons 25–28

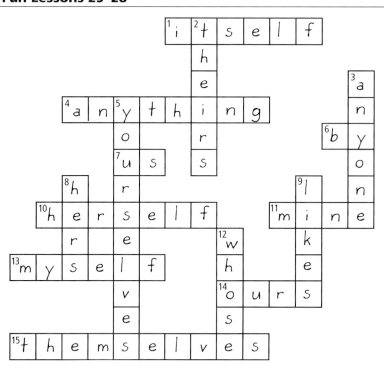

Lesson 29: Student Book

A

___ flashlights   ___ jackets   ✓ towel   ✓ soap   ___ sleeping bag
✓ toothbrushes   ___ toothpaste   ___ homework   ✓ book   ___ medicine

B

Singular Count Nouns	Plural Count Nouns	Non-Count Nouns
a towel	flashlights	soap
a book	jackets	toothpaste
a sleeping bag	toothbrushes	homework
		medicine

C

Kay: There's (1.) <u>a</u> good general **store** [SC] near here. They sell everything. What do we have to buy?

Ted: Well, we need (2.) Ø **toothpaste** [N] and (3.) <u>a</u> **flashlight** [SC]. Jenny's (4.) Ø **homework** [N] (is/are) at home, so there's nothing we can do about that.

Ted: True. What else do we need? It's so sunny here. I think Jenny needs (5.) <u>a</u> **hat** [SC] and (6.) Ø **sunscreen** [N].

Kay: Good idea. Hey—look over here. Free samples of (7.) Ø **chocolate** [N]!

Ted: Mmm. It (is/are) delicious.

Kay: And look! They sell (8.) Ø **pillows** [PC]. This store is amazing. I'd love (9.) <u>an</u> extra pillow. And I also need (10.) Ø **sunglasses** [N].

Ted: But Kay, these sunglasses (is/are) expensive. We need to save (11.) Ø **money** [N] for our tour of the national park tomorrow.

Lesson 30: Student Book

A

1. Laketown has (so many/**so much**) beautiful <u>scenery</u> [NC]. **T** F
2. There aren't (no/**any**) <u>movie theaters</u> [C] in Laketown. **T** F
3. I'll make (**a lot of**/much) <u>money</u> [NC] in Laketown. T **F**
4. Laketown has (**no**/any) <u>air pollution</u> [NC]. **T** F
5. I don't have (no/**any**) <u>friends</u> [C] in Central City. T **F**
6. There are only (a little/**a few**) <u>restaurants</u> [C] in Central City. T **F**
7. There aren't (**many**/much) cheap <u>apartments</u> [C] in Central City. **T** F
8. There's (**only a little**/only a few) <u>traffic</u> [NC] in Central City. T **F**
9. I don't have (many/**much**) <u>time</u> [NC] to make my decision. **T** F

B
1. Central City has <u>too much</u> crime. It's a little dangerous at night.
2. I love to go out to eat. There are <u>so many</u> restaurants there.
3. The streets are crowded. There are <u>too many</u> cars.
4. The air is terrible. Central City has <u>too much</u> pollution.
5. Central City is crowded. There are <u>too many</u> people.
6. I love Central City. I have <u>so much</u> fun there at night.
7. I love the excitement of Central City. There are <u>so many</u> things to do.

C
1. Central City has many restaurants.
2. Laketown has no museums.
3. Laketown has no pollution.
4. Laketown has many houses for rent.
5. Central City doesn't have any pollution.
6. People in Central City are busy. They don't have much free time.
7. Central City doesn't have any nice scenery.

Lesson 31: Student Book

A

I'm going to tell you (1.) <u>a</u> famous joke. Once upon a time, (2.) <u>a</u> mother mouse was running across (3.) <u>the</u> floor in the kitchen. (4.) <u>The</u> mother mouse was with her three children. Suddenly, (5.) <u>the</u> mother mouse heard (6.) <u>a</u> cat. (7.) <u>The</u> cat came into (8.) <u>the</u> kitchen. (9.) <u>The</u> baby mice were very scared. Then (10.) <u>the</u> mother mouse said, "Bow wow!" and (11.) <u>the</u> cat ran away. (12.) <u>The</u> mother mouse turned to her children and said, "See! I told you that it is very important to learn (13.) <u>a</u> foreign language!"

B

a—introduce noun	**the**—there is only one	**the**—the noun again	
<u>a joke</u>	<u>the floor</u>	<u>the mother mouse</u>	<u>the cat</u>
<u>a mother mouse</u>	<u>the kitchen</u>	<u>the mother mouse</u>	<u>the cat</u>
<u>a cat</u>		<u>the mother mouse</u>	
<u>a foreign language</u>		<u>the baby mice</u>	
		<u>the mother mouse</u>	

C
1. Once there was ~~the~~ <u>a</u> poor girl.
2. The poor girl's name was ~~the~~ Cinderella.
3. She lived in <u>an</u> old house with her stepmother and two mean sisters.
4. Every day, she cleaned <u>the</u> kitchen and cooked.
5. It was <u>the</u> hardest job in <u>the</u> world.
6. Then she met <u>a</u> prince at <u>a</u> big party.
7. The ~~P~~prince fell in love with her.
8. Her sisters wanted to marry <u>the</u> same man.
9. ~~A~~ <u>The</u> prince found Cinderella's house.
10. When she opened <u>the</u> door, he said, "Will you marry me?"

Lesson 32: Student Book

A

Well, I love (1.) hats [G]. I love big hats, small hats, berets, cowboy hats . . . all hats. (2.) The hat [Sp] that I'm wearing is from the 1940s. What do I dislike? Hmm. Well, I don't like (3.) spiders [G]. Spiders really scare me.

I love (4.) music [G]. My favorite music is (5.) jazz [G]. I don't like (6.) opera [G] very much. Opera is very difficult to understand. My aunt took me to (7.) an opera [Sp] once, and I fell asleep.

I love (8.) candy [G], especially chocolate. I think that (9.) chocolate [G] is good for you. I also love (10.) jellybeans [G]. Oh, I also love (11.) cute guys [G], especially my boyfriend. He's (12.) a really cute guy [Sp].

B

I love (1.) computers. My mother hates them, but I love them. My father bought me (2.) a computer last year. It's (3.) a wonderful computer. What do I dislike? Well, I dislike (4.) tests. We have (5.) a grammar test tomorrow, and I'm not happy about it. (6.) Tests make me nervous.

C

1. a. The snakes scare me.
   (b.) Snakes scare me.
2. a. The life is expensive here.
   (b.) Life is expensive here.
3. a. American house cost a lot.
   (b.) American houses cost a lot.
4. (a.) Children need exercise.
   b. Children need the exercise.
5. a. Motorcycle is dangerous.
   (b.) Motorcycles are dangerous.
6. a. I love fruit, especially the peaches.
   (b.) I love fruit, especially peaches.

Lesson 33: Student Book

A

Mark: It's a little cold here. Do you have (1.) (**another**/the other) table?

Waiter: Well, right now there are only two other free tables. One is near the door, and (2.) (another one/**the other one**) is over here, by the kitchen. Would you like that one?

Mark: Yes, we would. Thank you.

Waiter: We have two specials tonight. One is roast beef and (3.) (another one/**the other**) is salmon.

Linda: I'll have the roast beef. And, sir, could you please get me (4.) (another one/**another**/the other) glass? This one is a little dirty.

Waiter: Oh, I'm sorry. Certainly!

Linda: Mark, I have some important news.

Mark: What is it?

Linda: We're going to have (5.) (**another**/the other/the other one) baby!

Mark: Wow! That's great news!

Linda: I wonder if we'll have (6.) (**another**/other) son or (7.) (**another**/other) daughter. I'm so excited!

B

Not the last one(s). More are possible.	The last one(s). There are no more.
Do you have another table available?	One is near the door, and the other one is over here.
Could you please get me another glass?	
We're going to have another baby!	One is roast beef, and the other is salmon.
I wonder if we'll have another son or another daughter.	

C

1. Mark and Linda have two children. One is a boy, and <u>the</u> other one is a girl.
2. They have two children, and they want ~~other~~ <u>another</u> one.
3. One of their two children is five, and ~~another~~ <u>the other</u> one is three.
4. Their daughter doesn't want ~~other~~ <u>another</u> brother.
5. They already have a crib, but they need ~~another~~ <u>other</u> furniture for the new baby.
6. They have a stroller, but it's old. They will need to buy ~~the other~~ <u>another</u> stroller.

Review Lessons 29–33: Student Book

A

Lily: I don't know what to study, Dad.
Dad: I can give you some ideas. How about biology? You can be a doctor.
Lily: No, doctors have too much work. I want to have a lot of free time to travel around the world.
Dad: I have another idea. How about English? You can be an English teacher.
Lily: Or a reporter. Reporters travel a lot.
Dad: Some reporters do. But most reporters don't make much money, you know.
Lily: I read that the reporters on Channel 4 make $100,000 a year.
Dad: Not all of them do. Only two reporters there make a lot of money. One makes $100,000 and the other makes $95,000. You should really do what makes you happy.

B

	Quantity Word	+	Count Noun		Quantity Word	+	Non-Count Noun
1. I can give you	<u>some</u>		<u>ideas.</u>	3. I want to have	<u>a lot</u>	<u>of</u>	<u>free time</u> to travel.
2.	<u>Some</u>		<u>reporters</u> do.	4. No, doctors have		<u>too much</u>	<u>work.</u>
				5. But most reporters don't make		<u>much</u>	<u>money.</u>
	a/an		**Singular Count Noun**				***another/ the other(s)/other(s)***
6. You can be	<u>a</u>		<u>doctor.</u>	9. I have			<u>another</u> idea.
7. You can be	<u>an</u>		<u>English teacher.</u>	10. One makes $100,000 and			<u>the other</u> makes $95,000.
8. Or	<u>a</u>		<u>reporter.</u>				
General Statements				**Specific Statements**			
	Ø		**Plural Noun**		***The***		**Noun**
11. No,			<u>doctors</u> have too much work.	13. <u>The</u>			<u>reporters</u> on Channel 4 make $100,000 a year.
12.			<u>Reporters</u> travel a lot.				

C

1. His blue jeans ~~is~~ are ten years old!
2. Relax! We have ~~much~~ a lot of time.
3. Look! We have the same backpack.
4. I love you ~~too~~ so much!
5. I love classical ~~musics~~ music.
6. I don't like ~~bug~~ bugs.
7. We have ~~many homeworks~~ a lot of homework tonight.
8. There's a little traffic ~~a few traffics~~ today.
9. The ~~others~~ other students are in the library.
10. Can we rent another ~~movies~~ movie?
11. I have ~~many informations~~ a lot of information for you.
12. We need to buy ~~furnitures~~ furniture.
13. Can you give me some ~~an~~ advice?
14. My ~~another~~ other jewelry is at home.
15. There are four review exercises. We did three. Now, let's do the other exercise.

Have Fun Lessons 29–33: Student Book

A

Are you taking another class?	Are you taking two classes?	Do you eat too much candy?	Do you eat too many cookies?	Do you usually wear jeans?
Do you love chocolate?	Do you want a piece of chocolate right now?	Can you give me some advice?	Do you love apples?	Do you want an apple right now?
Did you have a lot of homework last night?	Do you have a lot of homework every day?	**Free Space**	Do you usually have too much homework?	Do you usually have too many assignments to do?
Do you like computers?	Do you have a computer?	Do you have a car and want another one?	Do you think there's too much traffic around here?	Do you think there are too many SUVs around here?
Do you like music?	Do you play a musical instrument?	Do you drink tea often?	Are you going to the supermarket this weekend?	Do you have some free time this weekend?

Lesson 34: Student Book

A

Juan: I think we should buy an SUV. It (1. is as big/(is as big as)) a minivan, and we can drive it anywhere.

Maria: But an SUV (2. isn't safe as/(isn't as safe as)) a minivan. SUVs roll over easily. We can get hurt. And a minivan holds more people.

Juan: Some SUVs carry (3.(as many)/as much) passengers as a minivan. And you know I like to drive fast. A minivan (4.(doesn't go as)/goes) fast as an SUV.

Maria: I don't care about speed. You know I don't drive (5.(as fast as)/as slow) you do. We have kids. I want a car that (6.(is as safe as)/isn't safe as) the one we have now. And we need space for our luggage on trips. An SUV doesn't have (7.(as much)/as many) space as a minivan. Also, SUVs are more expensive.

Juan: Well, an SUV has almost (8.(as much)/as many) space as a minivan. But you're right, we should get the minivan. I want you to be happy.

B
1. The food at Blues <u>isn't as good as the food at Rocky's</u>.
2. The waiters at Rocky's <u>are as friendly as the waiters at Blues</u>.
3. The servings at Blues aren't <u>as large as the servings at Rocky's</u>.
4. At Rocky's, they don't clean the tables <u>as well/often as they do at Blues</u>.
5. At Rocky's, they serve the food <u>as fast as they do at Blues</u>.
6. The prices at Rocky's <u>aren't as low as the prices at Blues</u>.
7. The music at Blues <u>isn't as loud as the music at Rocky's</u>.

Lesson 35: Student Book

A
1. Positive   (Negative)   5. Positive   (Negative)
2. Positive   (Negative)   6.(Positive)   Negative
3. Positive   (Negative)   7.(Positive)   Negative
4.(Positive)   Negative   8. Positive   (Negative)

B
1. Their new house is big enough.
2. Ryan doesn't live too far from his job.
3. Their neighbors aren't too noisy.
4. Ryan gets home early enough.
5. Ryan can spend enough time with the kids now.
6. There is enough space for their dog.

C

Question
Is your neighborhood safe enough?
Is your house or apartment too small?
Is your job close enough to your home?
Is your house or apartment too expensive?
Is your school close enough to your home?

Lesson 36: Student Book

A
1. <u>L</u>   It's more beautiful.
2. <u>SF</u> The buildings are newer.
3. <u>SF</u> The people seem less friendly.
4. <u>L</u>   Public transportation is more convenient.
5. <u>SF</u> The stores close earlier.
6. <u>L</u>   The roads are narrower.
7. <u>L</u>   The traffic is much worse.
8. <u>L</u>   The food is better.

B
1. Is your new job more interesting than your old job?
2. Is your English better now than it was before?
3. Who is more patient, your new boss or your old boss?
4. Is your new salary higher than your old salary?
5. Which apartment is closer to your work?
6. Are the people in your new neighborhood friendlier than the people in your old neighborhood?
7. Which apartment is older, this one or the other one?
8. Are the stores in your new neighborhood more expensive than the stores in your old neighborhood?

Lesson 37: Student Book

A

	East College	Central College	West College
the lowest tuition	✓		
one of the best music programs		✓	
the farthest from home		✓	
the least expensive dorms and food			✓
the highest tuition			✓
the biggest college		✓	
the most students		✓	
the fewest students			✓

B

Eric: Where can I meet people? I don't know anyone yet.
Josh: Well, one of (1.) <u>the easiest places</u> to meet people is Club 21. There's dancing and everyone is very friendly.
Eric: I need to find a cheap place to eat, too.
Josh: (2.) <u>The least expensive/cheapest restaurant</u> is The Pizza Factory. We all eat there. The food's good, too.
Eric: I also want to find a shopping mall. I don't have any winter clothes. I'm from California.
Josh: One of (3.) <u>the biggest malls</u> is downtown. Just take the streetcar. I'll show you. It also has a gym.
Eric: Is it (4.) <u>the best gym</u>? I'm very serious about working out.
Josh: It's not the best, but it's one of (5.) <u>the most popular gyms</u>.
Eric: Good. OK, one last thing. I need to register for a biology class. I need to pick (6.) <u>the easiest professor</u>.
Josh: None of the professors is easy. But Mr. Swan is (7.) <u>the friendliest</u>.

Review Lessons 34–37: Student Book

A

I need to talk to Amy about our vacation. One of the most relaxing places is Coast Island, but it's also one of the most expensive places. Santa Costa is almost as expensive, but we saved enough money for a nice trip. I don't want to go anywhere that's too far or too hot. For me, beach vacations are better than going to the mountains. That's because I'm very lazy, and all I want to do is just sit on a beach. My wife is much more energetic than I am, but she likes beaches, too.

B

1.
a. Coast Island is almost <u>as close as</u> Santa Costa.
b. Santa Costa is <u>as warm as</u> Coast Island.
c. Coast Island has <u>as many clubs as</u> Santa Costa.
d. Santa Costa has <u>as much entertainment as</u> Coast Island.
e. Vista Coast isn't <u>as expensive as</u> Coast Island.

2.
a. They think the trip to Coast Island is <u>too expensive/too long</u>, so they can't go there.
b. The weather in Vista Coast is <u>very</u> hot, but maybe they'll go there.
c. Vista Coast is <u>very</u> interesting, and they want to see the sights.
d. Jason says the flight to Coast Island is <u>too long</u>.

3.
a. The water in Vista Coast isn't <u>safe/clean enough</u> to drink.
b. They like to go out at night. There isn't <u>enough entertainment</u> in Vista Coast.
c. They don't have <u>enough money</u> to go to Coast Island, but they have almost <u>enough money</u> to go to Santa Costa.

4.
a. The trip to Coast Island is <u>more expensive than</u> the trip to Vista Coast.
b. The weather in Santa Costa is <u>better than</u> the weather in Vista Coast.
c. The weather in Vista Coast is <u>worse than</u> the weather on Coast Island.
d. Santa Costa is <u>farther than</u> Vista Coast.
e. The drinking water in Santa Costa is <u>cleaner/safer than</u> the water on Coast Island.
f. The Santa Costa beaches are <u>more beautiful than</u> the beaches on Coast Island.

5.
a. The trip to Coast Island is <u>the most expensive</u>.
b. Coast Island is the <u>farthest</u> from here.
c. <u>The longest</u> flight is to Coast Island.
d. Vista Coast has <u>the worst</u> weather.
e. Vista Coast has <u>the fewest</u> clubs.
f. Santa Costa has <u>the best/most beautiful</u> beaches.

Have Fun Lessons 34–37: Student Book

1. better
2. best
3. farther
4. farthest
5. worse
6. worst
7. less
8. least
9. sadder
10. hotter
11. bigger
12. noisier
13. easier
14. coldest
15. saddest
16. funniest
17. healthiest
18. newest

Secret message: My home is my castle.

Lesson 38: Student Book

A

Last summer, Jake and Cecilia Miller spent a week in the mountains. There <u>were</u> a lot of people <u>lying</u> on the beach by the lake. The sun <u>was shining</u>, and the water was clear blue. Everyone <u>was swimming</u>. But the Millers <u>weren't having fun</u>. They wanted some action. So, they rented a car to see the sights.

While they <u>were driving</u> along a narrow, curvy road, Cecilia <u>was taking</u> pictures, and Jake <u>was looking</u> for a station on the radio. He <u>wasn't paying</u> attention, and he hit a big hole in the road. He stopped the car immediately. When he got out to check the car, he saw that they had a flat tire. They were all alone. Cecilia <u>was beginning</u> to worry when a truck full of teenagers appeared. Luckily, they offered to help. While three of the teenagers <u>were changing</u> the tire, the others <u>were stopping</u> the other cars on the road.

Finally, the spare tire was on the car. Cecilia and Jake thanked the teenagers and drove back to their hotel. They were tired but ready for their next adventure.

B

Hi Greg,

We're having a great time on our vacation. But yesterday was a little scary. Cecilia (1.) <u>was taking</u> pictures and (2.) <u>talking</u> to me while I (3.) <u>was driving</u>, so I (4.) <u>wasn't paying attention</u> to the road. I hit a huge hole and got a flat tire. While I (5.) <u>was trying</u> to stop the car, Cecilia (6.) <u>was screaming</u>. Luckily, some kids stopped to help. While I (7.) <u>was helping</u> the kids change the tire, Cecilia (8.) <u>was crying</u> in the car. She's OK now, though.

Hi Betty!

We're having a lot of fun, but yesterday we had an accident. We (9.) <u>were exploring</u> the mountains. Jake (10.) <u>was driving</u> too fast and (11.) <u>looking</u> for a radio station. He (12.) <u>wasn't watching</u> the road and he hit a huge hole. We got a flat tire. Some kids (13.) <u>were driving</u> by and stopped to help us. While the kids (14.) <u>were changing</u> the tire, I (15.) was sitting calmly in the car. You know me. I don't really worry. I think Jake was really afraid. I hope the rest of the trip is better.

Lesson 39: Student Book

A

1. Was Lily walking across campus at 9:00? (Yes) No
2. Was Ana studying at the library at 9:00? Yes (No)
3. Was the teacher walking into the cafeteria at 9:30? (Yes) No
4. Was Singh eating in the cafeteria at 10:30? Yes (No)
5. Was Chen studying for the test in an empty classroom? (Yes) No
6. Was Ms. Kelly walking across campus at 11:00? Yes (No)

STUDENT BOOK ANSWER KEY   135

B
1. Was Ana eating in the cafeteria with Jon at 9:00?
2. What was Jon doing at 9:00?
3. Why was Chen studying for the test?
4. Was Jorge studying in the library?
5. Where was Jorge eating lunch?
6. Was Ming registering for a new class at 9:30?
7. When was Hoon swimming in the campus pool?

Lesson 40: Student Book

A

Susan and Daniel's wedding was last Saturday night. At 7:30, everyone (1.) <u>was sitting</u> and (2.) <u>waiting</u> for the bride and groom. Finally, they (3.) <u>came</u> in. While Daniel (4.) <u>was walking</u> down the aisle, his parents (5.) <u>were crying</u>.

After the ceremony, everyone (6.) <u>went</u> into the reception hall. While they (7.) <u>were dancing</u>, Daniel's father (8.) <u>stopped</u> the band because he (9.) <u>wanted</u> to make a toast. When the room was quiet, everyone (10.) <u>looked</u> at the couple. Daniel's father (11.) <u>held</u> up his glass and (12.) <u>wished</u> the newlyweds a long, happy, and healthy life together. Everyone (13.) <u>lifted</u> up their glasses and (14.) <u>said</u>, "I'll drink to that!"

B

PO: (1.) <u>Did you see</u> the accident?
Daniel: Yes, we did.
PO: What (2.) <u>were you doing</u> when the accident (3.) <u>happened</u>?
Susan: We (4.) <u>were buying</u> a newspaper when we (5.) <u>saw</u> it happen.
PO: What (6.) <u>did you see</u>?
Daniel: Well, at about 1:45, that woman over there (7.) <u>was crossing</u> the street. She (8.) <u>was carrying</u> a heavy bag and (9.) <u>walking</u> very slowly. The man in the black car (10.) <u>was waiting</u> for her to cross the street.
PO: What happened then?
Daniel: The white car suddenly (11.) <u>came</u> out of nowhere, and (12.) <u>hit</u> the back of the black car. There (13.) <u>was</u> a small explosion, and the black car (14.) started to burn. Both drivers (15.) <u>jumped</u> out of their cars. Luckily the car (16.) <u>stopped</u> burning quickly.
PO: (17.) <u>Did you see</u> anything else?
Daniel: No, that's about everything.
PO: Thank you. You've been very helpful.

Review Lessons 38–40: Student Book

A

It was a dark and stormy night. Eight hotel guests were sitting and talking by the fire. Some of them were drinking tea. Everyone looked worried. When lightening struck, everyone jumped. No one wanted to go upstairs to bed.

While the guests were talking, the hotel clerk came into the room and said, "Someone is at the door, and he is asking for Mr. Chambers." When he heard his name, Mr. Chambers didn't move. Everyone was looking at him, but he didn't get up. Then suddenly, . . .

B

(1.) It was a dark and stormy night. Eight hotel guests ⟨were sitting⟩ and ⟨talking⟩ by the fire. Some of them ⟨were drinking⟩ tea. Everyone looked worried. When lightening struck, everyone jumped. No one wanted to go upstairs to bed.

While the guests ⟨were talking⟩, the hotel clerk came into the room and said, "Someone is at the door, and he is asking for Mr. Chambers." When he heard his name, Mr. Chambers didn't move. Everyone ⟨was looking⟩ at him, but he didn't get up. Then suddenly, . . .

(2.) Any three of these are correct: was   looked   wanted   heard

(3.) NA Everyone *looked* worried.   A Everyone *was looking* at him.

D

Doctor: He'll be OK. Just let him rest.
Clerk: It was terrible. I (1.) was reading at my desk and everything (2.) was fine. The guests (3.) were talking and (4.) drinking tea by the fire. Then, when I (5.) heard the loud knock at the door, I almost (6.) fell out of my chair! I (7.) ran to the door and (8.) saw that young man. He (9.) wasn't very friendly. He (10.) came in and (11.) said he wanted to speak to Mr. Chambers. Poor Mr. Chambers. He (12.) was so shocked when he (13.) saw that young man. And I still don't know why!

Have Fun 38–40: Student Book

Various answers are possible.

Lesson 41: Student Book

A

Paula: Hi. I'm interested in a gym membership. A few months ago, my doctor recommended getting in shape and suggested going to a gym. I put off coming here, but finally, here I am!
Pete: Well, you're in the right place! What kind of exercise do you enjoy doing?
Paula: Well, none, actually. I always avoid exercising. I enjoy watching TV and reading.
Pete: Do you like to walk?
Paula: Well, I guess I don't mind walking. You know, a long time ago I used to jog.
Pete: That's great. Maybe you should consider using the treadmill.
Paula: Sounds good. Maybe I won't miss sitting around and watching TV after work!

B

get	getting	get up	getting up	eat	eating
use	using	live	living	spend	spending
be	being	watch	watching	tak	taking
work out	working out				

1. Paula enjoys getting exercise now. She loves her new lifestyle.
2. Paula avoids eating sweets and fatty foods.
3. She doesn't mind getting up early to go to the gym.
4. She enjoys watching TV in the evenings.
5. Paula can't imagine living without daily exercise.
6. She recommends using the treadmill.
7. She dislikes spending too much time at the office.
8. She is considering taking an exercise class.
9. She doesn't miss being lazy.
10. When she finishes working out, she takes a shower.

Lesson 42: Student Book

A

Most of the Chang family <u>had a great time camping</u> last week, but poor Harry Chang <u>had problems putting up</u> the tent. He <u>had fun reading</u> the instructions and <u>putting</u> the poles in the ground. But after that, he <u>had trouble holding up</u> the tent while he worked. Then he had a <u>hard time tying</u> the tent to the poles. He <u>spent two hours trying</u> and <u>trying</u>. Finally, he decided to go for a swim.

B
1. The kids are having a good time hiking.
2. Mary is having a hard time/trouble/problems pulling the cooler.
3. Mary is having fun/a good time/a great time catching fish.
4. Harry is having a hard time/trouble/problems fishing.
5. The kids are having a hard time/trouble/problems taking down the tent.
6. Harry is having fun/a good time/a great time reading.

Lesson 43: Student Book

A

Welcome to your first year at community college. During this orientation, we want to give you some helpful advice. <u>Keeping up with your work</u> (is) very important. If you get behind, it will be hard to get good grades. Also, <u>not getting enough sleep</u> (can be) a very serious problem. <u>Planning your schedule carefully</u> (will help) you find time to get enough sleep.

In addition, <u>saving time for relaxation</u> (will help) you do a good job at school. For instance, <u>seeing a movie with friends</u> (is) a perfect way to relax. <u>Going to college</u> (doesn't mean) that you never have fun.

Finally, <u>joining a study group</u> (will help) you study better. When students work together, they can help each other. <u>Joining student groups</u> (can help) you make new friends, as well. <u>Adjusting to college life</u> (can be) difficult, but if you follow these tips, it will be easier for you.

B
1. <u>Studying an hour or two every day</u> is important.
2. <u>Not getting a good night's sleep</u> will make it difficult to remember what you study.
3. <u>Keeping your notes organized</u> saves time.
4. <u>Is using the study labs on campus</u> helpful?
5. <u>Taking advantage of student services</u> is important.

Lesson 44: Student Book

A

Ana: How about Saturday for the party? People won't be (1. **tired**/tiring) from work.
Sarah: Perfect. You know, we need some (2. excited/**exciting**) activities for the kids so they won't be (3. **bored**/boring).
Ana: How about a piñata? They'll be (4. **excited**/exciting) to get candy and toys.
Sarah: Good idea! It'll be an (5. interested/**interesting**) party because our neighbors come from so many different countries.
Ana: True. It'll be great to get to know everyone, and it'll help us feel safer.
Sarah: Yeah, after those (6. frightened/**frightening**) robberies in the neighborhood last month, I'm (7. **frightened**/frightening) at night when my husband is away.
Ana: I know what you mean. We'll all feel so much more (8. **relaxed**/relaxing) when we get to know each other better. We can look out for each other.

B

Hi Cecilia,

We finally had our neighborhood street party last Sunday. It was an (1.) <u>exciting</u> day! Many people brought delicious and (2.) <u>interesting</u> food. The kids were (3.) <u>excited</u> by the piñata and music. I'm glad that none of them were (4.) <u>bored</u>.

It took a lot of work to organize the party with Sarah, but the party was very (5.) <u>relaxing</u>. Everyone sat around and talked, and I was (6.) <u>surprised</u> when I found out that there are people from seven different countries on my block!

You know, I was nervous about our new neighborhood, but now I feel much more (7.) <u>relaxed</u>. We have a great group of neighbors and I know we'll all watch out for each other. Now I'm not so (8.) <u>frightened</u> when Jorge works late.

Lesson 45: Student Book

A

Dear Annie,

I (1.) <u>'m attending</u> my last year of classes at my college. (2.) <u>Finding</u> a job that I really like worries me. Last year, I (3.) <u>was working</u> part-time at a software company while I (4.) <u>was taking</u> classes, but I wasn't happy. In fact, it was a very (5.) <u>boring</u> job. I realized that I like (6.) <u>working</u> with people more. Currently, I (7.) <u>am taking</u> a course called, "How to Teach Computer Literacy to Children." It's a very (8.) <u>interesting</u> class, and I love (9.) <u>being</u> with children. (10.) <u>I'm wondering</u> if I should stay in school longer. (11.) <u>Teaching computers</u> to children is what I really want to do. Is it too late to change direction?

B

Gerund Subjects	Gerund Objects	Continuous Verbs	-ing Adjectives
Finding	like working	am attending	boring job
Teaching	love being	was working	interesting class
		was taking	
		am taking	
		am wondering	

C

I (1.) <u>am writing</u> to say, "Congratulations!" You solved your own problem without my help. I'm so glad that you (2.) <u>are taking</u> a class in computers and teaching. Now you know what you want to do in the future. I recommend (3.) <u>staying</u> in school another year to take more classes in education. Last week, while I (4.) <u>was attending</u> a workshop, I learned that schools really need people like you. I am sure that you will have an (5.) <u>interesting</u> career. (6.) <u>Working with children</u> will be perfect for you.

Review Lessons 41–45: Student Book

A

At the end of a job interview, the interviewer usually asks if you have any questions. I recommend preparing a few questions ahead of time. Asking good questions can help you make a good impression. When you ask good questions, you show the employer that you are interested in the job. Not having questions prepared can be a problem. You'll have a hard time thinking of questions at the interview. I suggest asking what kind of employee does well at the company and what the most interesting part of the job is. However, you need to avoid asking about salary and vacations. That information will come later. Following my advice will bring you success—I'm sure of that!

B

Gerund Subject	Verb + Gerund	Adjective	
		-ing	-ed
Asking good questions	recommend preparing	interesting	interested
Not having questions prepared	have a hard time thinking		
Following my advice	suggest asking		
	avoid asking		

C

(1. G) Answering questions with, "yes" or "no" is not enough. (2. G) Giving explanations and details is a good idea. Also, show that you are (3. PC) enjoying (4. G) talking to the interviewer. Smile! Let the person know that you think the job sounds (5. A) exciting. And have confidence. Imagine (6. G) working there and (7. G) being successful. Let the interviewer know that you don't mind (8. G) working hard and that you consider (9. G) working there a dream come true. And finally, when you are (10. PC) sitting in the interview chair, think positive thoughts!

Have Fun Lessons 41–45: Student Book

A
1. I like <u>speaking</u> English.
2. I dislike <u>asking</u> for help or directions.
3. I don't mind <u>speaking</u> in front of a big group.
4. I can't imagine <u>giving</u> a speech in English in front of 100 people.
5. I avoid <u>speaking</u> my native language in class.
6. I'm considering <u>trying</u> some computer programs to learn English.
7. I enjoy <u>watching</u> TV in English.
8. I have a good time <u>doing</u> my homework.
9. I usually spend a lot of time <u>doing</u> my homework.
10. I have a hard time <u>remembering</u> spelling rules.
11. I'm having a problem <u>finding</u> time to work on my English.
12. <u>Understanding</u> a book or movie in English is exciting.
13. <u>Listening</u> to music helps me learn vocabulary.
14. <u>Watching</u> TV is good for my English.
15. <u>Being</u> successful is important to me.

Lesson 46: Student Book

A

Manuel: High school's finally over! I can't wait (1.) <u>to start</u> college in the fall. I want (2.) <u>to finish</u> quickly and go to medical school. I plan (3.) <u>to find</u> a cure for cancer and teach people (4.) <u>to be</u> healthy.

Yoshi: Are you crazy? School's over. We're finally free! I want (5.) <u>to work</u> in Europe, make money, and travel to Africa. I hope (6.) <u>to see</u> the world before I'm 25.

Manuel: How can you expect (7.) <u>to be</u> happy with no college education and no career?

Yoshi: I need (8.) <u>to be</u> free. That's what makes me happy.

B
1. Yoshi would like to work in Europe.
2. Yoshi can't afford to go to college.
3. Yoshi hopes to travel to Africa.
4. Yoshi can't wait to be free.

C
1. Manuel's parents want him to go to medical school.
2. Manuel's parents told him to be a responsible person.
3. Manuel needs his parents to help him pay for college.
4. Manuel's parents will help him pay for college.

Lesson 47: Student Book

A

Lena: Let's go to the beach! You can practice your driving. My sister and her boyfriend can help you. You're <u>lucky</u> (to get) this opportunity.
Elsa: You know I'm <u>afraid</u> (to drive) that far.
Lena: Well, it's not really that far, and it's <u>important</u> (to get) a lot of practice.
Elsa: I don't know. The roads to the beach are really narrow, and people drive so fast.
Lena: Yeah, that's true. But you're a really good driver already. Besides, it's <u>impossible</u> (to get) to the beach without a car, and you know I'm too <u>young</u> (to get) a license. If you practice now, we can go all the time.
Elsa: You're right. I am a good driver. And it will be <u>fun</u> (to practice) with your sister. Let's do it.

B
1. Elsa was afraid to practice driving too far.
2. It was fun to swim in the ocean.
3. It was not easy to drive on narrow roads.
4. Elsa was not excited to drive on narrow roads.
5. They were lucky to find a parking space.
6. Lena and Elsa were glad to walk on the beach.
7. Elsa was not afraid to swim in the ocean.
8. It was expensive to eat at the restaurant.
9. It was easy to get lost.
10. They were ready to go home at the end of the day.

Lesson 48: Student Book

A
1. b
2. d
3. c
4. e
5. a

B
1. Yes
2. Yes
3. Yes
4. Yes
5. No
6. No
7. Yes

Lesson 49: Student Book

A

Alex: This line is so long. I don't like (1. to wait/*waiting*) in long lines. I especially can't stand (2. to be/*being*) in line when it's so cold!
Tan: I know what you mean, but I really love (3. to see/*seeing*) movies.
Alex: Not me, I'm here for my kids. I prefer (4. to read/*reading*).
Tan: Really? I love (5. *to go*/going) to the movies, especially action movies. But my wife told me that I can't continue (6. *to take*/taking) the kids to those movies.
Alex: Why not?
Tan: Because they're so violent. She hates (7. *to let*/letting) the kids see all that violence.
Alex: She's right. I like (8. to take/*taking*) my kids to comedies. They won't have nightmares.
Tan: Oh look—the line started (9. to move/*moving*). Finally!

Review Lessons 46–49: Student Book

A

Toby is using Get-A-Date.com to look for a girlfriend. Last year, he was happy to meet Nicole online, and they dated for a while. But they decided to break up after six months. Toby thinks it's important to stay friends with Nicole, so they have dinner together once in a while.

But now Toby is 30. He wants to get married, and his parents want him to get married. It's difficult to find the right person, but he is trying. He began looking a few weeks ago, and he will continue looking until he finds her.

B

Verb + Infinitive	Verb + Object + Infinitive	Infinitive of Purpose	Verb + Gerund	Adjective + Infinitive
decided to break up	want him to get	to look for a girlfriend	began looking	happy to meet
wants to get			continue looking	important to stay
				difficult to find

C

1. Toby is using Get-A-Date.com to look for a girlfriend.
2. After six months, they decided to break up.
3. They have dinner once in a while because Toby thinks it's important to stay friends.
4. Toby's parents want him to get married.
5. He trying to find the right person.
6. He began looking a few weeks ago.
7. He will continue looking until he finds her.

D

Nicole is ready (1.) to get married. She wants (2.) to ask Danny (3.) to marry her. But she expects him (4.) to say, "No" because he's afraid (5.) to get married.

Nicole visited her sister (6.) to get advice. Her sister told her (7.) to be patient and wait. She told her (8.) to enjoy (9.) being with Danny right now, and she suggested (10.) waiting a few months before talking more about marriage.

That's going to be hard (11.) to do. Nicole has trouble (12.) keeping her feelings inside. She decided (13.) to talk to her old boyfriend Toby about this (14.) to get his advice.

F

1. Can you imagine using ~~to use~~ a service like this?
2. Some people postpone ~~to get~~ getting married, and then they are in a hurry to find someone.
3. Correct.
4. They suggest ~~to meet~~ meeting people through friends.
5. Even some people in their 70s know how to use online dating services.
6. Some services are expensive to use, and some are free.
7. People use these services ~~for~~ to meet others.
8. She doesn't want to meet~~s~~ people this way.
9. Some people are able to use ~~using~~ online dating successfully.
10. Do you plan to use ~~using~~ this kind of service?

Have Fun Lessons 46–49: Student Book

Various answers are possible.

Lesson 50: Student Book

A

My name is Katrina, and I'm 44 years old. I have two jobs and take care of my family. I go to school at night to learn English. It's hard for me to do all of the work for class. I try to turn (1. in/out) my homework on time, but sometimes I hand it (2. on/in) late. I try not to miss class because I know the teacher always passes (3. in/out) handouts, and I want to be there when she hands (4. it/them) out. I also need to be there to write (5. on/down) important information.

I'm always tired in class. Sometimes I don't understand the grammar lesson, and I have to figure it (6. on/out) at home. I look (7. out/up) new words in the dictionary, and sometimes I ask my son Frank to help me.

B

Katrina: Tom, did you turn in your homework?
Tom: (1.) Yes, Mom. I turned it in.
Katrina: (2.) Did you figure out your math problems?
Tom: Yes, Mom. I figured out my math problems.
Katrina: Did you make up your English assignment?
Tom: (3.) No, Mom. I didn't make it up.
Katrina: (4.) Did the teacher pass out the new science assignment?
Tom: Yes, Mom. The teacher passed out the new science assignment.
Katrina: Are you putting off writing your paper?
Tom: (5.) No, Mom. I'm not putting it off.
Katrina: Are you going to look up the addresses for the colleges you want to apply to?
Tom: (6.) Yes, Mom. I'm going to look them up.

Lesson 51: Student Book

A

Dear Fernanda,
Pablo's having a great time in Arizona. His first day of school was Monday. The boys got (1.) up early. They got (2.) on the bus near our house, and Pablo learned where to get (3.) off the bus when he goes to school by himself. At school, the teacher called (4.) on Pablo twice, and he answered in English

On Saturday, they ran (5.) into some of Carlos's friends and the boys stayed (6.) out all day and played. The two boys came (7.) back around seven o'clock. Then we all ate (8.) out at our favorite pizzeria. When we came home, Carlos's cousin dropped (9.) by, and the three of them listened to music and played computer games. Pablo will fit (10.) in well. Everyone seems to like him. I know I do!
    Maria

B

Phrasal Verb (no object)		Phrasal Verb (+ object)	
got up	ate out	got on the bus	called on Pablo
stayed out	dropped by	get off the bus	ran into friends
came back	fit in		

C

Fernanda: Maria says you (1.) fit in very well. I'm so proud of you!
Pablo: It's OK here. But my teacher (2.) calls on me a lot.
Fernanda: I know you don't like to talk in class. But when you (3.) come back to Mexico, you'll know English really well. Isn't that what you want?
Pablo: Yes, but I miss you and everyone. Mom, I want to (4.) get on a plane right now and fly home!
Fernanda: Oh, you're just a little homesick, Pablo. You'll (5.) get over it. Do you like spending time with Carlos?
Pablo: Sure. We have a great time. His friends (6.) come over a lot.
Fernanda: Well, that's great. And I know that Maria and Miguel (7.) look after you very well. You'll be fine.

Lesson 52: Student Book

A

    Do you dream about being out of high school? Do you look forward to being a college student or getting a job? Well, you're almost there.
    This year, you have some important things to do. You should concentrate on getting good grades because it's time to think about applying to college. Talk about your college possibilities with your family. And talk to your teachers and counselors. We'll listen to you because we care about your future. You can depend on us to help you.
    Also, don't forget about enjoying the senior activities. Try to participate in all of them. Most importantly, believe in yourself, and you'll succeed in reaching your goals.

B

about	to	in	on
dream	look forward	succeed	concentrate
care	listen	believe	depend
think	talk	participate	
talk			
forget			

C
1. Many students are listening <u>to the speech</u>.
2. Some students look forward <u>to going to college</u>.
3. Their parents are dreaming <u>of success</u> for their children.
4. The kids want to succeed <u>in/at getting</u> good grades.
5. They also want to participate <u>in senior activities</u>.
6. Some students are thinking <u>about/of getting advice</u>.

Lesson 53: Student Book

A
Lucy: Well, Mom, I'm all packed. I'm nervous (1.) <u>about</u> going, but I'm excited (2.) <u>about</u> my new job.
Mom: What are you nervous about? You're capable (3.) <u>of</u> doing anything you want. I'm so proud (4.) <u>of</u> you. You'll be fine, and this job is perfect (5.) <u>for</u> you. You're really good (6.) <u>at</u> what you do.
Lucy: Thanks, Mom. I'm sad (7.) <u>about</u> leaving my friends, but I'm happy (8.) <u>about</u> this new opportunity. I know I'll meet new people, and I'm interested (9.) <u>in</u> learning about this new company. I'll be responsible (10.) <u>for</u> a lot.
Mom: You'll be great. Now let's go. There's a lot of traffic, and you don't want to be late (11.) <u>for</u> your flight.

B

about	of	for	in	at
nervous	proud	late	interested	bad
sad	afraid	perfect	successful	good
excited	tired	responsible		successful
	capable	famous		

C
1. Lucy's boss says she's capable <u>of doing</u> a good job.
2. I'm not bad <u>at supervising</u> people.
3. I'm surprised <u>at the amount of work</u>.
4. Lucy feels proud <u>of herself</u>.
5. She's becoming famous <u>for being</u> a great cook.
6. The job seems perfect <u>for her</u>.
7. She isn't getting tired <u>of working</u> hard.

Review Lessons 50–53: Student Book

A
All day yesterday, I was looking forward to going to the theater after work. I was planning to eat out with my friend and then go to a really good show. When the elevator came, I was surprised by a noise it made, but I got on anyway. I was standing there and listening to someone's conversation when suddenly the elevator stopped. Everyone said, "Oh, no. Not again!" One guy said the elevator broke down last week. We were stuck in the elevator for three hours. I'm going to find out who's responsible for taking care of the building. I was very upset about missing dinner before the show.

B
1. Rosie was looking forward to going to the theater.
2. She was planning to eat out with her friend.
3. She was surprised by a noise the elevator made.
4. The elevator broke down.
5. She is going to find out who's responsible for taking care of the building.

C

Rosie and her friend stayed (1.) <u>out</u> late. After the show, they went to a cafe for a snack and ran (2.) <u>into</u> Rosie's old boyfriend Norman. Rosie used to care (3.) <u>about</u> Norman a lot. When they broke up, she tried to forget (4.) <u>about</u> him, but it was hard. At first, Rosie was nervous (5.) <u>about</u> talking to him, but she relaxed after a while. Rosie and her friend talked (6.) <u>to</u> Norman for around an hour, and they were interested (7.) <u>in</u> hearing his news. While they were talking, Rosie suddenly realized that Norman was perfect (8.) <u>for</u> her friend.

D
1. Everyone looked forward to <u>getting</u> ~~get~~ out of the elevator.
2. Everyone was interested in <u>getting</u> ~~to get~~ off.
3. Correct.
4. Their phones didn't work in the elevator, so they put ~~away~~ them <u>away</u>.
5. She dropped her phone and someone picked ~~up~~ it <u>up</u>.
6. The fire department succeeded <u>in</u> getting everyone out safely.
7. They were responsible for ~~to take~~ <u>taking</u> care of everybody.
8. Rosie only cared about <u>getting</u> ~~get~~ to the theater on time.
9. She didn't eat out, but she wasn't late <u>for</u> ~~at~~ the show.
10. At the theater, she didn't get ~~it~~ in the elevator. She walked up the stairs.

E
1. eats <u>out</u> once a week — Do you eat out once a week?
2. ate <u>out</u> last Saturday night — Did you eat out last Saturday night?
3. gets <u>up</u> late on Sunday mornings — Do you get up late on Sunday mornings?
4. always turns homework <u>in</u> on time — Do you always turn homework in on time?
5. puts <u>off</u> studying for tests — Do you put off studying for tests?
6. usually writes <u>down</u> what the teachers says — Do you usually write down what the teacher says?
7. frequently drops <u>by</u> friends' houses — Do you frequently drop by friends' houses?

Have Fun Lessons 50–53: Student Book

Various answers are possible.

Lesson 54: Student Book

A
1. Rika (might have/**has**) a new neighbor.
2. Rika's new neighbor (is/**could be**) at work a lot.
3. He (is/**might be**) very busy.
4. He (**could be**/is) a doctor or a policeman.
5. He (**keeps**/might keep) his curtains closed.
6. He (**doesn't open**/might open) his windows in hot weather.
7. He (likes/**may like**) peace and quiet.
8. He (is/**could be**) 40 or 50.
9. He (**has**/might have) some gray hair.

B
1. The new neighbor might ~~works~~ underline{work} at night.
2. He could ~~to~~ be a doctor.
3. He may not underline{have} ~~has~~ a job.
4. The new neighbor might ~~to~~ be a policeman.
5. He might not underline{be} a doctor.
6. Rika and Jon may underline{meet} ~~meeting~~ him soon.

Lesson 55: Student Book

A
1. He (is/**must be**) well trained.
2. He (**must eat**/eats) well.
3. He (likes/**must like**) kids.
4. Rika's sister and brother (**want**/must want) to keep the dog.
5. His owner (is/**must be**) very upset.
6. The dog (must belong/**belongs**) to someone else.
7. The dog (must not have/**doesn't have**) a name tag.
8. He (isn't/**must not be**) very old.
9. Rika (**is thinking about**/must be thinking about) putting up signs in the neighborhood.

B
1. The dog looks tired. He <u>must not sleep</u> enough.
2. The dog looks very clean. Someone <u>must take</u> care of him.
3. He acts very friendly. He <u>must like</u> people.
4. He keeps looking out the window. He <u>must be</u> homesick.
5. He's pretty big. He <u>must not be</u> a puppy.
6. He's running in circles. He <u>must want/like</u> to play.

C Possible answers:
1. The baby must be tired/unhappy/and hungry.
2. They must be married/happy.
3. He must like hamburgers/be hungry.
4. He must not like vegetables/broccoli/must not be hungry.
5. They must have a test tomorrow/must be nervous.
6. They must not be at home.

Lesson 56: Student Book

A
    Francisco was born in the United States. Next month he's going to visit Argentina for the first time. Francisco's parents are from Argentina, and he wants to meet his relatives. He's a little nervous because he has a lot to do before he goes. He (1. <u>has to</u>/doesn't have to) renew his passport for the trip because it expired, but he (2. <u>doesn't have to</u>/has to) get a visa. He doesn't need a visa to go to Argentina.
    His mother told him that he (3. <u>should</u>/shouldn't) take gifts to his relatives because they like to get presents from the United States. It's winter in Argentina in July, so he (4. <u>shouldn't</u>/should) take summer clothes. He (5. <u>has to</u>/doesn't have to) take warm clothes. He (6. <u>doesn't have to</u>/has to) make hotel reservations because he can stay with relatives. His mom said he (7. should/<u>shouldn't</u>) take a lot of cash. Instead, he (8. <u>should</u>/shouldn't) take his ATM card. He knows he (9. <u>should</u>/shouldn't) go to bed early the night before the flight because it's a long trip.

B

I'm Diego, Francisco's cousin. We had a great time last July when he visited Argentina, and now I'm planning to visit him in San Diego. He told me I (1.) should visit him because he lives in a city with my name. Then I told him that we (2.) should take a trip to San Francisco because his name is Francisco!

Before I go, I need to work on my English. I signed up for an English class, but I missed the first class because I (3.) had to work. When I went to the second class, the teacher gave me some advice. She said, "You (4.) should choose between work and school." Well, I (5.) have to work to save money for my trip, so I decided to study English on my own.

There's a café in the city where people practice their English. Since I (6.) didn't have to work last Friday, I went and talked to a tourist from Los Angeles for about an hour. It was great! I asked her a lot about California. Now I know I (7.) should rent a car in San Diego because it's a big city, but I (8.) shouldn't rent a car in San Francisco because it's hard to park there.

Lesson 57: Student Book

A
1. Now
2. Later
3. Later
4. Later
5. Now
6. Now
7. Now

B
1. What type of lease does Jim have to sign?
2. Should he call the cable company to connect his TV?
3. When should he change his address?
4. Does he have to pay a deposit?
5. What furniture does he have to buy?
6. Where should he look for a truck to rent?
7. Should he reserve a truck?

Lesson 58: Student Book

A
Tran: Hi, Susana. How are you? I'm so happy to (1. see/seeing) you!
Susana: Tran! You look great! What are you (2. do/doing) these days?
Tran: Well, you know, I used to (3. be/being) a gymnastics teacher. But last year I decided to (4. open/opened) my own gym.
Susana: Wow! That's terrific! I should (5. go/to go) to your gym. I need some exercise.
Tran: I hope you do! So, what's new with you? Did you (6. graduate/graduated)?
Susana: Yes, last month. Now I'm (7. look/looking) for a job in a hospital.
Tran: I'm sure you'll (8. get/to get) a job soon.

B
1. Do Tran and Susana (know) each other?
2. What did Tran (decide) to (do)?
3. What does Susana (want) to (do)?
4. Did Tran used to (have) a job?
5. Should Susanna (join) Tran's gym?
6. Why should Susanna (join) Tran's gym?

C
1. Maki: Hi Susana. Where did you go ~~went~~ today?
2. Susana: Downtown. And guess what? I saw our old classmate Tran! **C**
3. Maki: I remember Tran. He used to be ~~being~~ a gymnastics teacher.
4. Susana: That's right. Well, last year he decided to open ~~opened~~ his own business.
5. Maki: That's very exciting. Does he live ~~lives~~ near here?
6. Susana: I don't know. I wanted to ask ~~asked~~ him that question, but I didn't ~~had~~ have time.
7. Maki: I would like to see him. **C**
8. Susana: Well, you can visit him at his new gym. It's downtown. **C**
9. Maki: We should go ~~going~~ together.
10. Susana: Good idea! **C**

Review Lessons 54–58: Student Book

A
Bill: Hey, Bob! You shouldn't throw those newspapers away.
Bob: I know. I should recycle them, but I don't know how.
Bill: Ask your landlord. There must be some recycling containers around here.
Bob: I looked, but I didn't see any.
Bill: They might be behind that wall. I'll check...Yup! There they are. I knew it! See—you have to look around and ask questions when you move in.
Bob: I know. But you know how shy I am. Thanks for helping me out.

B
1. Does Bob have ~~has~~ to recycle?
2. He used to recycle ~~recycling~~ at his other apartment.
3. Where ~~he~~ should he put the newspapers?
4. He has ~~have~~ to help the environment.
5. Bill must care ~~cares~~ about the environment.
6. Does he recycle ~~recycles~~ glass too?
7. There might not be a place to put the newspapers.
8. He had to clean ~~cleaned~~ his apartment.
9. He didn't have ~~had~~ to help his brother.
10. Correct
11. Bill can ~~to~~ help his brother.
12. Bill wants to help ~~helps~~ Bob.
13. Bill was happy to help ~~helped~~ Bob.

C Possible answers:
1. What's wrong? He must be late for class.
2. What is he? He could be a student because he looks young.
3. What should he do? He should get out of the rain.
4. What does he have to do? He has to stop.
5. How is he? He must be really hungry.
6. What should he do? He should clean his living room.

Have Fun Lessons 54–58: Student Book

Various answers are possible.

Lesson 59: Student Book

A

Kevin wants to learn more about his family, so he <u>has spent</u> some time interviewing his grandmother. His grandmother <u>has had</u> an interesting life. She <u>has been</u> married for 40 years. She <u>has been</u> a mother for 35 years. She <u>has had</u> five different jobs, and she <u>has worked</u> at her present job for the last ten years. She <u>has been</u> a waitress, a teacher, and the director of a school. She <u>has lived</u> in many houses during her life, and she and Kevin's grandfather <u>have lived</u> in this house for over 20 years. She <u>has learned</u> to ski, snowboard, and scuba dive. She <u>has been</u> an artist and a gardener, too.

B

love	loved	learn	learned	go	gone
have	had	sleep	slept	know	known
read	read	fly	flown	try	tried
see	seen	visit	visited	be	been

1. Grandma <u>has learned</u> five languages.
2. Grandma <u>has had</u> her job for ten years.
3. Kevin and his sister <u>have flown</u> in a small airplane with Grandma.
4. Grandma <u>has slept</u> on a mountain in a tent.
5. Kevin and his sister <u>have read</u> many books about traveling.
6. Kevin and his sister <u>have eaten</u> many kinds of interesting food with Grandma.
7. Grandma <u>has been/has gone</u> around the world and <u>(has) seen</u> lots of famous places.
8. Grandma <u>has known</u> and <u>(has) loved</u> Grandpa for 42 years.

C

Base Form	Past	Past Participle
write	wrote	written
eat	ate	eaten
stop	stopped	stopped
speak	spoke	spoken
need	needed	needed
get	got	gotten
make	made	made
carry	carried	carried
do	did	done
want	wanted	wanted
take	took	taken

Lesson 60: Student Book

A

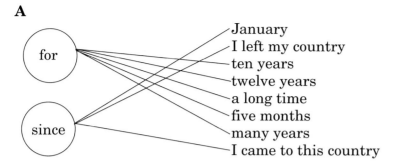

B

Alberto has worked for Denise (1.) <u>for</u> six months, and he's learned a lot about her. Denise has been in the U.S (2.) <u>for</u> 20 years. She's lived in Boston (3.) <u>since</u> 1993. Denise loves working in her beauty salon. She's worked in the beauty business (4.) <u>for</u> over 20 years and she's owned her own salon (5.) <u>since</u> 1995. Denise and her husband haven't been back to Argentina (6.) <u>for</u> ten years and she hasn't seen her family (7.) <u>since</u> 1995. Denise and her husband hope to return for a visit soon. Their youngest child has finished high school and has been in college (8.) <u>for</u> a year and a half. Denise is happy to have Alberto working for her because she hasn't taken any days off work (9.) <u>since</u> March, and she needs a break.

Lesson 61: Student Book

A

| climb—<u>climbed</u> | take—<u>taken</u> | go—<u>gone</u> |
| jump—<u>jumped</u> | be—<u>been</u> | |

1. Has Ted ever <u>been</u> on a roller coaster? (Yes, he has.) No, he hasn't.
2. Has Ted ever <u>gone/been</u> surfing? Yes, he has. (No, he hasn't.)
3. Has Ali ever <u>climbed</u> a mountain? (Yes, he has.) No, he hasn't.
4. Has Ali ever <u>jumped</u> out of a plane? (Yes, he has.) No, he hasn't.
5. Has Ted ever <u>taken</u> a hot air balloon ride? Yes, he has. (No, he hasn't.)

B
1. Has Ted ever traveled alone? Yes, he's traveled alone a few times.
2. Has Ali ever driven to the mountains? Yes, he's often driven to the mountains./ Yes, he has driven to the mountains often.
3. Have Ted and Ali ever been to L.A.? Yes, they've been to L.A. once.
4. Has Ted ever gone surfing? No, he's never gone surfing.
5. Have Ali and Ted ever taken a trip together? Yes, they've taken a trip together a couple of times.
6. Has Ali ever gotten sick on a roller coaster? Yes, Ali has gotten sick on a roller coaster once.

Review Lessons 59–61: Student Book

A

Have you ever (fallen) in love at first sight? Well, I never have. I know it happens in the movies. My cousin always falls in love immediately, but she has (been) married and divorced three times! You know what? She's in love again, and she has (known) the guy [for] only two weeks. She has (been) this way [since] she was a teenager. My brother has (tried) to give her advice, but she doesn't listen. Oh well. I hope she has (found) the right guy this time.

B
1. A
2. B
3. B
4. A
5. A

C

My twin cousins always fall in love immediately, but they have been married and divorced three times! You know what? They're in love again and they have known the guys for only two weeks. They have been this way since they were teenagers. My brother has tried to give them advice, but they don't listen. Oh well. I hope they have found the right guys this time.

D
1. Has Robert ever won the lottery?
2. Has his life changed a lot?
3. Has his family been on TV?/Has his family ever been on TV?
4. Has he given his family many presents?
5. Has he spent money only on himself?
6. Has he helped his community?

E
1. has
2. is
3. has
4. is
5. is
6. has

F
1. ~~Have~~ Has he met many people?
2. Since I came ~~have come~~ to the U.S., I've met a lot of people.
3. We have been in school ~~since~~ for two years.
4. They have rarely had free time ~~rarely~~.
5. She has never spoken English with her children ~~never~~.
6. They've never ~~be~~ been on an airplane.
7. I have ~~learn~~ learned a lot.
8. Has he ever gone to the city ~~ever~~?

G
1. He hasn't seen his family since 2018.
2. She has been on vacation for two weeks.
3. I haven't spoken English for two days!
4. We have been in this room since 10 a.m.
5. They have had a lot of work since last Tuesday/since August 11.
6. I've known her for eight years.
7. You've been absent since August 8th.
8. It has been very cold for two days.

Have Fun Lessons 59–61: Student Book

A

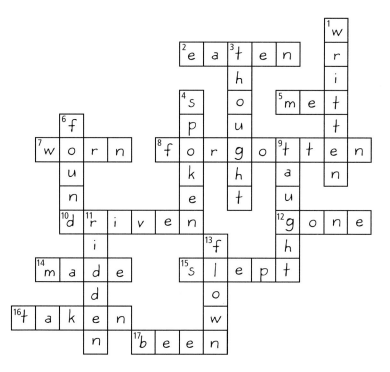

Lesson 62: Student Book

A

	Things Victor has already done	Things Victor hasn't done yet
registered for classes	✓	
bought his books		✓
joined the International Students Club	✓	
called Eva		✓
told Eva about his new girlfriend		✓

B
1. Q: <u>Has Victor made new friends yet?</u>
   A: Yes, he's already made several new friends.
2. Q: <u>Has Victor tried the new cafeteria yet?</u>
   A: No, he hasn't tried it yet.
3. Q: <u>Why hasn't Victor tried it yet?</u>
   A: Because he brings his lunch from home.
4. Q: Has Victor joined any clubs yet?
   A: <u>Yes, he has already joined two clubs.</u>
5. Q: <u>Has Victor been to any parties yet?</u>
   A: Yes, he's already been to several parties.
6. Q: Has Victor had any exams yet?
   A: <u>No, he hasn't had any exams yet.</u>
7. Q: <u>Why hasn't Victor had any exams yet?</u>
   A: Because he has been in school for only one month.
8. Q: <u>Has Victor seen Eva yet?</u>
   A: Yes, he's seen her a few times.

C Possible answers:
Has Victor set the table yet? No, he hasn't set the table yet.
Has Victor chosen music yet? No, he hasn't chosen music yet.
Have Victor and Chang gone shopping yet? No, they haven't gone shopping yet.
Have Victor and Chang cleaned the house yet? No, they haven't cleaned the house yet.
Have Victor and Chang decorated the apartment yet? Yes, they have already decorated the apartment.
Has Chang washed the dishes yet? Yes, Chang has already washed the dishes.
Has Chang put the pizza in the oven yet? No, Chang hasn't put the pizza in the oven yet.
Has Chang bought flowers yet? No, Chang hasn't bought flowers yet.

Lesson 63: Student Book

A

Soccer Experiences	How Long?	How Many Times?
has played on the school team (Kim)	for five years	
has played goalie (Kim)	for five years; since his first year	
has won games (Kim)		10 times
has traveled for a game this year (Kim)		20 times
has been to games (Pedro)		6 times
has played soccer (Pedro)	for two years	

B
1. (How long/How many times) have you played tennis?
2. (How long/How many times) have you seen your favorite soccer team?
3. (How long/How many times) have you been interested in sports?
4. (How long/How many times) have you gone/been bowling?
5. (How long/How many times) have you played volleyball?
6. (How long/How many times) have you run/been in a marathon?
7. (How long/How many times) have you been a baseball player?

Lesson 64: Student Book

A

Julia and Tao are new classmates. They started their English class three days ago. They've spoken to each other a few times and have learned many things about each other. Julia moved here three years ago from El Salvador with her family. She has attended several English classes and her English has improved. So, last month she decided to look for a job. She has had some job interviews, and she hopes to find a job soon. Julia and her family have made many friends here.

Tao's experience has been very different. He arrived two months ago from China, and he came alone. His brother didn't come with him, and he's very sorry about that. He's made only one friend, so he's very lonely. Tao found a good apartment two weeks ago, and he has gotten some furniture. But he hasn't bought a TV yet. Julia has told him that things will get better soon and that he has to be patient.

B

Natasha: Oh Julia, I'm so glad we have a few minutes to talk. (1.) <u>Have you had</u> any job interviews yet?

Julia: Uh-huh. I (2.) <u>have had</u> three since I (3.) <u>saw</u> you at Andy's house. But I (4.) <u>have not heard</u> anything yet.

Natasha: I (5.) <u>had</u> a job interview yesterday. They (6.) <u>offered</u> me the job right away, but I (7.) <u>didn't take</u> it because it's too far away. I told them yesterday.

Julia: I'm sure you'll find something soon. (8.) <u>Have</u> you <u>moved</u> into your new apartment yet?

Natasha: Uh-huh! I (9.) <u>moved</u> in two weeks ago. I (10.) <u>have met</u> a few of my neighbors already. And last weekend, one of them (11.) <u>invited</u> me to dinner. I (12.) <u>had</u> a great time.

Julia: That's great. Well, I have to go. Good luck with the interviews. I know you'll get a good job!

Review Lessons 62–64: Student Book

A

Interviewer: Thank you for letting me interview you.
Mr. Wilson: No problem. We're always happy to give interviews.
Interviewer: How many times have you given interviews before?
Mrs. Wilson: Oh, five or six in the last ten years, I think. We're happy to talk about our lives.
Interviewer: That's great. So tell me, you're both 101 years old, right?
Mr. Wilson: That's right.
Interviewer: And how long have you been married?
Mrs. Wilson: Ahhh...We've been happily married for 79 years.
Interviewer: Have you started planning a party yet for your 80th anniversary?
Mrs. Wilson: No, *we* haven't, but two of our great grandchildren have. They have already reserved a restaurant.
Mr. Wilson: But they haven't sent out the invitations yet.
Mrs. Wilson: Don't worry, dear. They will.
Interviewer: And here's another question...

B

1. How long has Mrs. Wilson been married?
2. Have they given the guest list to their great-granddaughter yet?
3. Why haven't Mr. and Mrs. Wilson given her the list yet?
4. How many interviews have they given in the past ten years?

C

A few weeks ago, I (1.) <u>interviewed</u> my great-grandparents for many hours. I (2.) <u>asked</u> them a lot of questions about their travels, and I (3.) <u>learned</u> a lot. Last week, I (4.) <u>made</u> a DVD of our interview so our family will always have our history. I (5.) <u>have already made</u> about 30 copies of the DVD to give as birthday presents to different members of our family.

When I interviewed my grandparents, they (6. tell) <u>told</u> me that they (7.) <u>have had</u> wonderful lives. They (8.) <u>have known</u> each other since they (9.) <u>were</u> kids, and they (10.) <u>have been</u> married for almost 80 years!

Their life together (11.) <u>has been</u> very interesting. They (12.) <u>have traveled</u> all over the world and (13.) <u>have met</u> people from many different cultures. When they (14.) <u>were</u> in Italy in the summer of 1952, they (15.) <u>taught</u> English and (16.) <u>studied</u> Italian. They (17.) <u>lived/have lived</u> in India, China, Congo, and Brazil, too!

D

b, f, g 1. Jackie has been a filmmaker
a, c, d 2. She got interested in the career when she met her husband
b, e, f, g 3. They haven't made a film together
a, c, d 4. They talked about making a film together
a, c, d 5. They met at work
b, f, g 6. They have been married

a. a few years ago.
b. for a few years.
c. in 2014.
d. a long time ago.
e. yet.
f. since 2016.
g. since she graduated from college.

Have Fun 62–64: Student Book

Various answers are possible.

Expansion Activities Answer Key

Lesson 1: Expansion Activity

A

Benjamin is ~~an~~ a young man. He is from Mexico. Now he lives in Brasilia. His two sisters live with him. He has one younger brothers in Mexico. Benjamin works in a ~~factories~~ factory in Brasilia. He has many friends. His best friend's name is ~~joao~~ Joao.

Lesson 2: Expansion Activity

Various answers are possible.

Lesson 3: Expansion Activity

A

My name is Abeer. I came here from Bangladesh 12 years ago. I studied English for two years and then entered a university. I ⟨didn't⟩ have much money, but I got a scholarship. I majored in computer science. I graduated, and now I'⟨m⟩ working as a computer programmer. I'⟨m⟩ not married, but I ⟨am⟩ going out with Paloma, a young woman from Mexico. We ⟨are⟩ getting married next year. We ⟨will⟩ move to Chicago because there are many programming jobs there. I miss Bangladesh, and Paloma misses Mexico, but we want to stay in the U.S.

Lesson 4: Expansion Activity

A

Adjective	Adverb	Adjective	Adverb
careful	carefully	fluent	fluently
fast	fast	early	early
clear	clearly	slow	slowly
good	well	smooth	smoothly
late	late	hard	hard

B Possible answers:
1. Kim works as a receptionist in a/an American/Korean/large/big/small/important company in Seoul, Korea.
2. She speaks Korean, Japanese, and English well/fluently/badly.
3. She is a good/careful/bad/slow/fast worker.
4. At night, she takes business classes at a university. She studies hard/carefully.
5. She is doing well/badly in her classes.
6. On the weekends, she is usually too tired to go out with her friends.
7. She tries to exercise and eat well because she knows she needs to stay healthy.
8. Once a year, Kim takes a long/short/expensive vacation with her friends.

Lesson 5: Expansion Activity

A

Pierre lives <u>in</u> Paris. He works <u>in</u> a large office building <u>from</u> 9:00 <u>to</u> 5:00. He drives <u>to</u> his office every day. <u>In</u> his car, he often listens <u>to</u> classical music <u>on</u> the radio. <u>In</u> the evening, Pierre goes home and waits <u>for</u> his daughter Monique to get home <u>from</u> school. Last summer, Pierre and Monique traveled <u>across</u> the United States together. They drove <u>through</u> some beautiful areas, including the Grand Canyon. They also drove <u>around</u> New York and Boston, their two favorite cities. The traveled <u>for</u> four weeks then returned <u>to</u> France.

Lesson 6: Expansion Activity

A
1. This is my brother Tran. <u>He</u> lives in California with his wife Karen.
2. <u>This</u> is my sister May. She lives with my parents in Canada.
3. These are my grandparents. <u>They</u> are Canadian citizens now.
4. They live in Toronto. <u>It</u> is a beautiful city.
5. My sister and I want to see each other this year. <u>We</u> miss each other.
6. This is my brother Li. <u>He</u> lives in California, so he sees Tran a lot.

Lesson 7: Expansion Activity

A
1. Sandra is confused <u>because</u> she has two boyfriends.
2. She can't decide who to date. Mark is handsome, <u>but</u> John is nice.
3. Sandra was angry at Mark <u>because</u> he didn't remember her birthday.
4. Last week, John called Sandra <u>and</u> bought her flowers.
5. John is nice to Sandra, <u>so</u> she likes him a lot.
6. Will she go to the dance with Mark, <u>or</u> will she go with John?

Lesson 8: Expansion Activity

Various answers are possible.

Lesson 9: Expansion Activity

Various answers are possible.

Lesson 10: Expansion Activity

A
1. I often have problems with English.
2. Lynn and Janet sometimes call each other.
3. They meet for coffee once a week./Once a week, they meet for coffee.
4. Right now, they are listening to Mylo singing.
5. Are they practicing tonight?
6. They always spend New Year's Eve together.

Lesson 11: Expansion Activity

A
Dear Annie,

My name <u>is</u> Andy. I attend high school now, but I'm entering college next September. I <u>want</u> to study English literature because I <u>love</u> poetry, and I am thinking about studying poetry someday. My parents <u>think</u> that it<u>'s</u> a bad idea. They <u>want</u> me to study engineering or business so that I will have a comfortable life. I really <u>disagree</u> with them. I'm having trouble talking to them. What should I do?

Lesson 12: Expansion Activity

A
1. travel — traveled
2. visit — visited
3. buy — bought
4. want — wanted
5. make — made
6. miss — missed
7. have — had
8. go — went
9. come — came
10. catch — caught
11. do — did
12. decide — decided
13. fall — fell
14. use — used

Lesson 13: Expansion Activity

Various answers are possible.

Lesson 14: Expansion Activity

A
1. Are you going to go to the party tomorrow?
2. No, I will probably be with Martine.
3. When is she leaving for Brazil?/When is she going to leave for Brazil?
4. She's going to leave the day after tomorrow.
5. Will she stay there a long time?
6. Correct.

B
1. Is Martine going to go to Brazil next month?
2. She is going to watch Brazil's national soccer team.
3. Does she think that Brazil will win?
4. She probably won't come back home soon.

Lesson 15: Expansion Activity

A Possible answers:
1. Yes, I'll be your best man.
2. No, I won't. I need the money for college.
3. Don't worry. You'll be a wonderful couple!
4. I promise I won't be late./I'll be on time.
5. I'll pick up the flowers.
6. I'll take you to the airport.
7. It will probably rain tomorrow.
8. I hope that she won't be late.

Lesson 16: Expansion Activity

A

My name is Karl. I just started a computer company in Germany. <u>If business is good this year</u>, I will have to travel a lot next year. That will be hard for my family and me. <u>If I have to spend a lot of time in other cities</u>, I won't see my family very much. I will have to change something <u>if I have to keep traveling</u>. My family is too important to me! <u>After I get more business</u>, I'll hire an assistant. <u>When there is a sales trip</u>, my assistant will go instead of me. <u>Before I make enough money to hire an assistant</u>, though, I will have to do all of the traveling. <u>When I am traveling</u>, I will call my family and talk to them as much as possible. That will help us all feel better. <u>If business is good this year</u>, I will hire the assistant next year. That will solve my problem!

Lesson 17: Expansion Activity

B

Lim: I need a ride to the airport tomorrow.
Rick: I'll take you. What time does your flight leave?
Lim: (1. leave/noon) It leaves at noon.
Rick: No problem. We can leave at 10:00.
Lim: But I have to stop at the drugstore before my flight. I have to pick up a prescription.
Rick: What time does the drugstore open?
Lim: (2. open/10:00) It opens at 10:00.
Rick: OK. So we should leave here at 9:30.
Lim: And I have to drop off my dog Jacko at the kennel. They're taking care of him.
Rick: Well, what time does the kennel open?
Lim: (3. open/9:00) It opens at 9:00.
Rick: Maybe we should leave here at 8:30, then.
Lim: That sounds good. You know I'm a little worried about how I'm going to get to my brother's house once I arrive.
Rick: What time does your flight arrive?
Lim: (4. arrive/midnight) It arrives at midnight.
Rick: That's really late. When does the airport shuttle stop?
Lim: (5. stop/1:00 a.m.) It stops at 1:00 a.m.
Rick: You can take the shuttle, then. No problem.

Lesson 18: Expansion Activity

A

1. Was Lee born in the United Kingdom?
2. Did Lee and his sister grow up in Asia?
3. Does Lee like studying English?
4. Is Lee going to stay here?
5. Will he be sad when the semester is over?
6. Are his parents traveling in England now?
7. Did they teach Chinese at Cambridge University?
8. Were they good teachers?
9. Do they teach now?
10. Did Lee and his sister meet them in Paris last year?

Lesson 19: Expansion Activity

Various answers are possible.

Lesson 20: Expansion Activity

A

1. James always does his best.
2. Does he work hard at school?
3. He always does his homework.
4. He doesn't sleep late on Saturdays./On Saturdays, he doesn't sleep late.
5. Did he study hard in high school?
6. He did very well in high school.
7. Does he do the dishes after dinner?
8. John's roommate doesn't do anything around the house.
9. Yesterday, he didn't clean his room./He didn't clean his room yesterday.
10. He didn't do the dishes.

Lesson 21: Expansion Activity

A
1. Who is your best friend?
2. Who do you live with?
3. Who did you talk to yesterday?
4. Who is Martin going to go to the movies with this weekend?
5. Who is with Martin right now?
6. Who did Charlene spend the weekend with?

Lesson 22: Expansion Activity

Various answers are possible.

Lesson 23: Expansion Activity

A Possible answers:
1. Aren't you tired? Don't you want to stay home tonight?
2. Don't you have homework?
3. Why don't you take an aspirin?
4. Didn't he move to New York?/Doesn't he live in New York?
5. Don't you usually work late on Mondays?

Lesson 24: Expansion Activity

A
1. Katrina <u>isn't</u> a very good swimmer. She can't hold her breath under water.
2. Katrina <u>didn't/couldn't</u> go to the pool yesterday because it was closed.
3. She <u>doesn't/shouldn't/can't/won't</u> swim right after she eats lunch.
4. She could dive very well when she was five years old, but now she <u>can't/doesn't</u> dive well.
5. She knew all of the different swimming strokes at one time, but now she <u>doesn't</u> know them all.
6. She wanted to go to Hawaii for Christmas, but she <u>couldn't/didn't</u> go because she was sick.
7. Her friends are having a party tonight, but she <u>won't/can't</u> be there because she's still feeling bad.
8. Katrina's parents wanted to go to a movie, but they <u>aren't</u> going to go because they're worried about Katrina.

Lesson 25: Expansion Activity

A
Kim: I really like 1. <u>our</u> apartment.
Lee: I do too. 2. <u>Its</u> ceilings are really high, and it has great views.
Kim: And 3. <u>your</u> bedroom is great! I like it better than 4. <u>mine</u>.
Lee: It's too bad that 5. <u>our</u> living room is so small.
Kim: Yeah, and I don't like 6. <u>its</u> carpet.
Lee: June and Viggo have a great apartment! 7. <u>Their</u> living room is really big.
Kim: Yeah. It's much bigger than 8. <u>ours</u>.
Lee: But at least 9. <u>our</u> view is better than 10. <u>theirs</u>.

Lesson 26: Expansion Activity

A
1. I saw her last night at the jewelry store.
2. She liked it very much.
3. When she put it on, she said to me, "It's very beautiful!"
4. After a while, she bought them.
5. They looked very good on her.
6. After she bought the necklaces, she showed them to him.

Lesson 27: Expansion Activity

Various answers are possible.

Lesson 28: Expansion Activity

A
1. I don't know anything about the people in my class.
2. Everybody else is always having fun.
3. I don't have any money to travel during vacations.
4. I'm not going to go anywhere for New Year's Eve.
5. I'm not doing anything interesting.
6. Next year, I'm going to do something to change my life!
7. Sometimes I feel that no one likes me.

Lesson 29: Expansion Activity

Count Nouns	
flashlight	knife
sleeping bag	belt
boot	tent
shoe	apartment

Non-Count Nouns	
information	homework
sand	water
jewelry	music
weather	coffee
butter	sugar
furniture	equipment
	fun

Lesson 30: Expansion Activity

Various answers are possible.

Lesson 31: Expansion Activity

A
Juan: What's your neighborhood like?
Ali: Well, it's really nice. It's on the side of (1.) a big hill.
Juan: Can you see much from your house?
Ali: Yes, there is (2.) an excellent view.
Juan: What can you see?
Ali: You can see (3.) a big lake and (4.) a beautiful forest. (5.) The lake usually has sailboats on it.
Juan: What's in the neighborhood?
Ali: Well, there are mostly just houses. But there is (6.) an office building and (7.) a shopping center, as well. (8.) The shopping center has two good restaurants.
Juan: Where do you work?
Ali: I work in (9.) the office building.
Juan: What else is there in your neighborhood?
Ali: Well, there's (10.) a large park with many trees.
Juan: Your neighborhood sounds wonderful!

Lesson 32: Expansion Activity

My name is Brian. I live in Topeka, Kansas, but I'm traveling around Europe now. It's difficult moving around so much, but I have all of my clothes in <u>a</u> big backpack. That really helps. I'm amazed by the sights, the food, and the people of Europe. I generally love <u>Ø</u> monuments and <u>Ø</u> museums, and there are a lot of them in Europe. <u>The</u> museums in Paris are the best. The Louvre is incredible. I always look for <u>Ø</u> good food and <u>the</u> food is great here. I love <u>Ø</u> pasta, especially <u>the</u> pasta in Italy. The variety of sauces is amazing! Everywhere I go, I always try to meet <u>Ø</u> people. Today, I met <u>a</u> very nice Italian man who was interested in Kansas. Europeans often meet people from New York and Los Angeles, but never from Kansas. <u>Ø</u> life in Europe is very stimulating. I may move here some day.

Lesson 33: Expansion Activity

1. Frank and his brother Bob are always fighting over things. There were three pieces of apple pie. Bob ate two of them. Frank ate (the other ones/<u>the other one</u>).
2. Bob had four small pieces of chocolate. He gave two pieces to Frank. Frank wanted (<u>another one</u>/the other).
3. Frank and Bob's mother baked two cakes, a big one and a small one. She gave them the small cake. They were unhappy because they wanted (other/<u>the other one</u>).
4. Frank and Bob are in a skateboard club with Jorge, Steven, and Mary. Jorge called Frank and Bob and asked them to go skateboarding. Frank said, "OK, but let's call (the other/<u>the others</u>)."
5. Frank and Bob went to a movie on Saturday afternoon. When it was over, Bob said, "Let's go see (<u>another one</u>/the other one)."
6. After the second movie, Frank said, "I really liked that movie." Bob said, "I didn't like it. I liked (another one/<u>the other one</u>)."
7. Frank and Bob visited their aunt and uncle in Georgia. Their aunt and uncle have eight children. Six are boys; (the other/<u>the others</u>) are girls.
8. After they went to Georgia, the boys visited (<u>another</u>/another one) aunt in Florida.
9. Their aunt in Florida has two sons. Frank and Bob didn't like one, but they really had fun with (<u>the other</u>/another).
10. When they got back home, they told Jorge, Steven, and Mary about their travels. Jorge was really interested in their stories, but (the other one/<u>the others</u>) were bored.
11. Steven and Mary wanted to go to the park, but Jorge said, "I want to hear (<u>another</u>/the other) story about Georgia."

Lesson 34: Expansion Activity

A
1. My sedan is not as large as my minivan.
2. My son is not as tall as my daughter.
3. Our dog weighs almost/nearly as much as our neighbors' dog.
4. Our rent is as high as my sister's rent.
5. I'm not as unhappy as I used to be.
6. I'm nearly/almost as old as my wife.

Lesson 35: Expansion Activity

A
1. This is a nice party, but the music is (<u>too loud</u>/loud enough). I can't hear what anyone is saying.
2. There are a lot of people here. It's a good thing that Melinda's house is (<u>big enough</u>/too big).
3. I have to leave in a little while. I hope I have (<u>enough time</u>/too much time) to talk to my friends.
4. I just ate some pastries that were delicious. The food at this party is (<u>very good</u>/too good).
5. More people are still coming in to the party. It's getting (crowded enough/<u>too crowded</u>) here.
6. I just talked to Todd. He's (too nice/<u>very nice</u>).
7. I'll have to take a bus home. It's (far enough/<u>too far</u>) to walk.
8. Buses aren't fast, but they're (<u>reliable enough</u>/too reliable) to get me home safely.
9. I would ask Andre for a ride, but he drives (fast enough/<u>too fast</u>)!
10. Taxis are convenient, but they're (expensive enough/<u>too expensive</u>).
11. I don't have (<u>enough money</u>/too much money) for a taxi.

Lesson 36: Expansion Activity

A

bad	<u>worse</u>	big	<u>bigger</u>	busy	<u>busier</u>	expensive	<u>more expensive</u>
far	<u>farther</u>	fast	<u>faster</u>	good	<u>better</u>	modern	<u>more modern</u>
new	<u>newer</u>	pretty	<u>prettier</u>	sad	<u>sadder</u>	strong	<u>stronger</u>

B Possible answers:
1. The weather is better in Florida than in New York City.
2. Florida is warmer than New York and has more beautiful beaches.
3. Housing in Florida is cheaper than in New York.
4. Apartments in New York are more difficult to find and more expensive than in Miami.
5. Miami is less crowded than New York.
6. The museums in New York are more interesting than in Miami.

Lesson 37: Expansion Activity

A

bad	<u>the worst</u>	big	<u>the biggest</u>	busy	<u>the busiest</u>
expensive	<u>the most expensive</u>	far	<u>the farthest</u>	fast	<u>the fastest</u>
good	<u>the best</u>	late	<u>the latest</u>	less	<u>the least</u>
new	<u>the newest</u>	sad	<u>the saddest</u>	small	<u>the smallest</u>

Lesson 38:

A

Ruth: Bret, the beach party last night was great! Where were you?
Bret: (1.) <u>I was visiting my brother</u>.
Ruth: You were at Brad's house? I thought that he was in Italy.
Bret: (2.) <u>Yes, he was studying cooking in Italy</u>. He got back last week.
Ruth: Is he a good cook now?
Bret: He's excellent! (3.) <u>Last night I was watching while he was cooking spinach pie and pasta</u>. It was incredible. So the beach party was great?
Ruth: Yes. It was fantastic! The weather was perfect. (4.) <u>The waves were crashing on the beach, and a gentle breeze was blowing</u>. (5.) <u>A lot of people were dancing</u>. (6.) <u>Other people were talking and eating Mexican food</u>.
Bret: What kind of music were they dancing to?
Ruth: (7.) <u>A live band was playing salsa</u>.
Bret: Sounds great!
Ruth: (8.) <u>Motoki and Juana were walking along the beach together all evening</u>.
Bret: Really? Now that is news!

Lesson 39: Expansion Activity

Various answers are possible.

Lesson 40: Expansion Activity

A

When I <u>was</u> born, my family (was living) in a rural part of western Brazil. It <u>was</u> incredibly beautiful, but we <u>were</u> quite close to the jungle. One day, I (was playing) with my older brother in the backyard. We (were digging) holes in the ground and (building) castles with stones. While we (were playing), I <u>heard</u> something behind me. I <u>looked</u> up and <u>screamed</u>. A jaguar (was coming) towards us slowly. Luckily, my grandmother (was working) in the garden with a big rake. She <u>ran</u> straight at the jaguar with the rake. It <u>ran</u> back into the jungle. Soon after that, we <u>moved</u> to a city.

Lesson 41: Expansion Activity

Various answers are possible.

Lesson 42: Expansion Activity

A
1. Ibrahim had a hard time finding a good campsite.
2. Nancy had a good time/had a great time/had fun camping.
3. Paloma had a hard time/had trouble/had problems building a fire.
4. Ibrahim had a hard time/had trouble/had problems sleeping on the hard ground.
5. Mathew spent four hours finding enough firewood.
6. Joshua had a hard time/had trouble/had problems hiking eight miles yesterday.
7. Barney had a good time/had a great time/had fun swimming in a mountain lake.
8. They had a hard time/had trouble/had problems starting the car.
9. They spent six hours driving home.

Lesson 43: Expansion Activity

Various answers are possible.

Lesson 44: Expansion Activity

A

     I went to an (1. <u>amazing</u>/amazed) party last week. I met two very (2. <u>interesting</u>/interested) people, Frank and Billy. Frank is a musician who plays the trumpet. He's a (3. <u>fascinating</u>/fascinated) man. He plays (4. <u>exciting</u>/excited) jazz that's really fast. He thinks slow jazz is (5. annoyed/<u>annoying</u>). I'm (6. amazing/<u>amazed</u>) by his energy. Billy is very different from Frank, as he is very (7. relaxing/<u>relaxed</u>). At the party, he looked as if he felt (8. boring/<u>bored</u>), but he didn't. I had a (9. <u>stimulating</u>/stimulated) conversation with him. He spends a lot of time reading and thinking. He thinks philosophy and literature are very (10. interested/<u>interesting</u>). For me, reading philosophy is really (11. <u>boring</u>/bored), but I loved listening to Billy talk about it.

Lesson 45: Expansion Activity

A

1. Last week, I went to a workshop on careers in aviation. Now, I <u>am thinking</u> about becoming a pilot.
2. It was very crowded. People <u>were standing</u> at the back of the room.
3. A woman led the workshop. She said, "<u>Becoming</u> a pilot is a great dream to have."
4. Everyone thinks that it's a very <u>exciting</u> job.
5. However, <u>being</u> a pilot is difficult.
6. My uncle is a pilot. Right now, he <u>is flying</u> a route from Cleveland, Ohio to Atlanta, Georgia.
7. Before that, he <u>was flying</u> from Reno to Dallas.
8. When he was young, he lived in Paris. <u>Living</u> in Paris again some day is his dream.
9. He loves <u>eating</u> French food.
10. He only takes a few vacation days a year. He <u>is working</u> hard for his future.
11. Right now, his pilot job is quite <u>boring</u>.

Lesson 46: Expansion Activity

A

     When I was younger, my parents <u>wanted me to go</u> [VOI] to medical school. They saved up all of their money and <u>planned to pay</u> [VI] for my college. They <u>expected me to study</u> [VOI] biology and chemistry. I followed their plan for one year, but then I told them that I hated science. I <u>loved to read</u> [VI] great literature, and I <u>didn't want to be</u> [VI] a doctor. I <u>tried to convince</u> [VI] them that being a doctor wasn't for me. They finally understood and <u>allowed me to change</u> [VOI] my major. I am now a professor of literature at a small college in Oregon. I have a son. I <u>want him to read</u> [VOI] great books, but he <u>would like to be</u> [VI] a doctor. My parents are very happy with him. I'm happy that he knows what he wants.

Lesson 47: Expansion Activity

Various answers are possible.

Lesson 48: Expansion Activity

A

I'm a good decision-maker when it comes to career choices, but when it comes to relationships and marriage, I need some help. I chose to come to Chicago <u>to find</u> a good job. Then I chose to study English <u>to get</u> an even better job. I chose to be a computer engineer <u>to earn</u> a lot of money. Now I have a really good job and am saving money <u>to buy</u> a house. My next big choice is about marriage. I'm seeing someone I really care about but am not sure if I should ask her to marry me. I know that you have to be really in love <u>to propose to someone</u>. I don't want to do it just <u>to please</u> my family or anyone else. Can you give me some advice?

Lesson 49: Expansion Activity

A

Joan: Do you like <u>going</u> to movies?
Lin: I love <u>seeing</u> movies! What kind do you like?
Joan: I like <u>to watch</u> Chinese movies the best, but I can't stand <u>going</u> to Chinese martial arts movies.
Lin: Really? Well, *Red Thunder* is playing at the Centerville Theater. It's not far from here. Let's start <u>walking</u>. It'll take about ten minutes.
Joan: Great idea! After the movie, let's go to dinner. What kind of food do you like?
Lin: Well, I recently started <u>going</u> to that new Thai place on Sutter Street. It's really good.
Joan: Thai food is OK, but I prefer <u>eating</u> French or Italian food.
Lin: OK, let's have Italian then. I love <u>to eat</u> pasta.

Lesson 50: Expansion Activity

A

1. Motoki's boss passed it out to the team.
2. Motoki had to look it over for his boss.
3. At first, he put it off.
4. Then, he looked them over.
5. He wrote them down.
6. He looked them up in a grammar book.
7. He finally figured them out.
8. He handed it in yesterday.
9. He found it out this morning.
10. Today, the boss handed it out.
11. Motoki wants to give it back tomorrow.

Lesson 51: Expansion Activity

  I <u>grew up</u> in a very small rural community. There wasn't much to do, but I had fun with my friends. I always <u>got up</u> early in the morning to help my mother make breakfast. On school days, I had to <u>get on</u> (the bus) around 7:00 in the morning and ride for ten miles. I <u>got off</u> in Dade City. I <u>came back</u> home around 3:30. My parents were still at work, so my grandmother <u>looked after</u> (me.) I often ate a snack and then <u>dropped by a friend's house</u>. It was a very small community, so we were always <u>running into</u> (friends.) I sometimes ate dinner at a friend's house. There were no restaurants in my community, so nobody ever <u>ate out</u>. My friends and I sometimes had no homework, so we <u>stayed out</u> until sunset. After dark, there wasn't anything to do, so I always just <u>went back</u> home.

Lesson 52: Expansion Activity

A

1. In high school, I participated in many activities.
2. When I started high school, I was really looking forward to graduating.
3. I believed in the value of education, but I wanted to be free.
4. It was difficult for me to concentrate on my studies.
5. My father told me that I should care about my studies more.
6. He and my mother dreamed of having a doctor in the family.
7. I listened to their advice.
8. Correct.
9. Now, I am starting to succeed in my classes.
10. I look forward to being a university student.
11. In the future, I will always depend on my parents for good advice.

Lesson 53: Expansion Activity

A

  I am interested (1.) <u>in</u> the bookkeeper position at your company and would like to schedule an interview with you. I am now working for a small grocery store as a bookkeeper. I am excited (2.) <u>about</u> the idea of working for a larger company. In my current job, I am responsible (3.) <u>for</u> paying all of the bills and the employees' salaries. I am an excellent employee and am never late (4.) <u>for</u> work. I am very good (5.) <u>at</u> handling money. I was successful (6.) <u>at</u> cutting costs in the store, but I am capable (7.) <u>of</u> doing much more. I believe that I am perfect (8.) <u>for</u> the position. Please contact me at (869) 555-9520 to schedule an interview.

EXPANSION ACTIVITIES ANSWER KEY

Lesson 54: Expansion Activity

A

Vic: Good afternoon, Patricia. Thanks for coming over for lunch.
Patricia: It's my pleasure. Where's Leonard?
Vic: I don't know. He was going to drive here. He's very late.
Patricia: (1.) <u>There could be a traffic jam.</u>
Vic: I was driving around a little while ago. There didn't seem to be any problems. But he has a very old car.
Patricia: (2.) <u>He may/could/might be stuck somewhere.</u>
Vic: Yes, that's a possibility. But you know, I just moved here last month. He doesn't even know my new address.
Patricia: (3.) <u>He may/could/might be at your old house.</u>
Vic: Oh, I hope not. How will he find us?
Patricia: (4.) <u>He may/could/might call you on his cell phone.</u>
Vic: Yeah, that's what he'll probably do.
Patricia: (5.) <u>He may/could/might arrive soon.</u>
Patricia: Yes, you're right.
Vic: Look over there. Something strange is happening.
Patricia: What do you mean?
Vic: There's a man climbing into that window.
Patricia: (6.) <u>That may/could/might be his house.</u>
Vic: Why doesn't he use the door?
Patricia: (7.) <u>He may/might not have his key.</u>
Vic: No, I know the people there. He doesn't live there.
Patricia: (8.) <u>He may/could/might be a burglar.</u>
Vic: (9.) <u>The police may/might/could come soon.</u>
Patricia: Yes, but let's call them anyway.

Lesson 55: Expansion Activity

A

Sarah: I had a really interesting day. I walked around the city. In the morning, I walked by that new house on the corner. A family was moving furniture into it.
Jaime: They (1.) <u>must be</u> the owners.
Sarah: That's what I thought. They have a lot of expensive furniture!
Jaime: They (2.) <u>must be</u> rich.
Sarah: I agree. They were carrying in a lot of toys, too.
Jaime: They (3.) <u>must have</u> children.
Sarah: I saw a lot of dolls and cute dresses, but nothing for boys.
Jaime: They (4.) <u>must not have</u> any sons.
Sarah: Then I went downtown. On Main Street, I saw Mary's store. Somebody broke the window in her pastry shop.
Jaime: Mary (5.) <u>must be</u> really angry!
Sarah: Yes, she *is* really angry. And the person stole all her best pastries.
Jaime: That person (6.) <u>must like</u> pastries a lot!
Sarah: I think so, too.
Jaime: Did you see Mary's daughter?
Sarah: Yes, she looked really tired. She said that college is really difficult.
Jaime: She (7.) <u>must have</u> a lot of homework!
Sarah: Yeah. She's always working.
Jaime: Well, you (8.) <u>must be</u> tired after your busy day.
Sarah: Yes, I am. I'm going to rest. I'll talk to you later.

Lesson 56: Expansion

B
1. My brother should study harder.
2. He has to study tonight because he has a test tomorrow.
3. My parents have to talk to him about his studies.
4. Correct.
5. He should go to college because he is very intelligent.

Lesson 57: Expansion Activity

A
1. When do you have to apply to colleges?
2. Why do you want to go to Central City College?
3. Should you talk to the counselor at school?
4. Do you have to get good grades this year?
5. Who has to write letters of recommendation for you?
6. Should we apply for financial aid soon?
7. Should your friend Jose apply to good schools because of his excellent grades?
8. Why do you have to get a job?
9. Will you have to live in the dormitory your first year?
10. When do you have to get up tomorrow morning?

Lesson 58: Expansion Activity

A

Dad: Mary, did you (1.) <u>have</u> a good day today?
Mary: Yes, Dad. I (2.) <u>had</u> a really nice day.
Dad: Really? That (3.) <u>'s/is</u> great!
Mary: Yeah, I (4.) <u>ran</u> into Arnold in the park.
Dad: He (5.) <u>'s/is</u> such a nice man. Does he still (6.) <u>work</u> at the bank?
Mary: No, he used to (7.) <u>work</u> there, but he's a student now. He (8.) <u>'s/is studying</u> for a master's degree in business.
Dad: That's wonderful! He will (9.) <u>do</u> really well. I should (10.) <u>call</u> him to say, "Hi."
Mary: Well, he's going to (11.) <u>come</u> over for dinner Saturday night.
Dad: I'm really happy to (12.) <u>hear</u> that. You two used to (13.) <u>be</u> such good friends in high school.
Mary: I know. I'm glad I ran into him. You know, it must (14.) <u>be</u> difficult for him to (15.) <u>find</u> time to study. He has to (16.) <u>work</u> on the weekends.
Dad: I can't imagine (17.) <u>getting</u> a master's degree while working. But he's young! He'll (18.) <u>be</u> OK! I'm really looking forward to (19.) <u>seeing</u> him again!
Mary: Me, too.

Lesson 59: Expansion Activity

A
1. Martha's mother and father <u>have been married</u> for 25 years.
2. Martha's brother <u>has climbed</u> Mount Everest twice.
3. Martha <u>has lived</u> in five different countries.
4. Martha's sister <u>has been</u> the CEO of a large corporation.
5. Martha's grandmother <u>has learned</u> five languages.
6. Martha's grandfather <u>has written</u> three novels.
7. Martha's father <u>has invented</u> three machines.
8. Martha's family <u>has done</u> many remarkable things.

Lesson 60: Expansion Activity

A

Dear Aunt Grace,

    I'm really sorry that I <u>haven't written</u> you (1.) <u>for</u> so long. I <u>have lived</u> in Montreal, Canada (2.) <u>for</u> four years and my life here is really busy. When I first arrived, I studied English for a few months. After living in Canada for one year, I got a job at McKay Imports. I <u>have worked</u> for them (3.) <u>since</u> then. They liked my work a lot and promoted me. I <u>have been</u> a manager (4.) <u>for</u> two years. The company asked me to start an M.B.A. program at McGill University. I <u>have taken</u> night and weekend classes (5.) <u>for</u> a year and a half. Studying and working at the same time is difficult, but I really want the degree. I'm going to finish my M.B.A. next year.

    I <u>have known</u> a wonderful Canadian man named Karl (6.) <u>for</u> two years. We <u>have been</u> married (7.) <u>since</u> last December. We bought a house in January and <u>have lived</u> in it (8.) <u>for</u> three months. We even bought a dog! We <u>have had</u> Fluffy (9.) <u>for</u> two weeks.

    Do you remember my younger sister Kathy? She <u>has lived</u> with us (10.) <u>since</u> March. She <u>has worked</u> (11.) <u>since</u> last month as an accountant. She <u>has studied</u> English at night (12.) <u>since</u> she arrived.

    We really love Canada, except for the winter, of course, and we hope that you'll visit us soon.

Lesson 61: Expansion Activity

Various answers are possible.

Lesson 62:

Jane: Jonas, <u>have</u> you <u>packed</u> your bags?
Jonas: (No, Mom, I haven't.) I'm going to do it tonight.
Jane: <u>Have you bought</u> a new suitcase?
Jonas: (Yes, I have.) It's right here.
Jane: It's beautiful, Jonas. <u>Have</u> you <u>brought</u> the old trunk up from the basement?
Jonas: (Yes, I have.) It's downstairs. I have to clean it this afternoon.
Jane: <u>Have you told</u> all of your friends your new address?
Jonas: (Yes, I have.) I told everyone at my going away party last night.
Jane: That's good. <u>Has</u> Dad <u>bought</u> you a bus ticket for tomorrow? He sometimes forgets things these days.
Jonas: (Yes, Mom. He has.) But he <u>hasn't given</u> me the address of his old friend in New York. He wanted me to visit him.
Jane: I'll remind him. His friend Andy can help you a lot when you first get there. Well, we'll miss you, son.
Jonas: I'll miss you too, Mom.

Lesson 63: Expansion Activity

A

Erik: Alice, (1.) <u>how long</u> have you been a surfer?
Alice: I've been a surfer (2.) <u>for</u> three years.
Erik: How did you learn to surf?
Alice: Well, at first I taught myself, but I've had a teacher (3.) <u>since</u> last year. That's helped a lot.
Erik: Where do you usually surf?
Alice: I usually go to Ocean Beach because there are always waves.
Erik: (4.) <u>How long</u> have you surfed there?
Alice: I've surfed there (5.) <u>for</u> about two years.
Erik: (6.) <u>How many times</u> have you surfed at Mavericks?
Alice: I've gone there five times. I like it, but the waves are so huge that I usually just watch. I've only actually surfed there once.
Erik: This is a nice surfboard. (7.) <u>How long</u> have you had it?
Alice: I've had it (8.) <u>for</u> two years. It's in bad condition now. I should buy another one for Hawaii. I'm going there next month.
Erik: (9.) <u>How many times</u> have you been to Hawaii?
Alice: I've never been there before. This will be my first time.
Erik: I'm sure it'll be exciting. (10.) <u>How many times</u> have you been to Florida?
Alice: I've been to Florida two times. It was quite lovely. My sister is there now.
Erik: (11.) <u>How long</u> has she been there?
Alice: She has been there (12.) <u>since</u> February.
Erik: Well, it has been great talking to you.

Lesson 64: Expansion Activity

A

Dear Mom and Dad,

Things are going OK here in Barcelona. I (1.) <u>arrived</u> two weeks ago and (2.) <u>have found/found</u> a nice family to live with. I have a small room with a bath. The family doesn't speak English, so I (3.) <u>'ve spoken</u> only Spanish with them so far. My school is on the other side of the city, so yesterday, I (4.) <u>bought</u> a bus pass to get to school. School (5.) <u>hasn't started</u> yet, but I (6.) <u>'ve made</u> several friends already. Since I met my new friends, I (7.) <u>'ve visited</u> many beautiful places in the city with them. Two days ago, we (8.) <u>went</u> to see a beautiful cathedral, and yesterday, we (9.) <u>drove</u> with some friends to the beach. Two days ago, I (10.) <u>saw</u> Mario. Do you remember him? He (11.) <u>told</u> me to say, "Hello," to you. He (12.) <u>'s been</u> an accountant for the Spanish government for a year now, but he doesn't really like his job. Well, I need to study some more. I'll write again.

Review Tests Answer Key

Review Test: Lessons 1–5

A
1. <u>noun</u>   Carla won a <u>trip</u> to Hawaii.
2. <u>adverb</u>   She learned English <u>fast</u>.
3. <u>verb</u>   She <u>wrote</u> an excellent composition.
4. <u>preposition</u> The weather was perfect <u>in</u> Hawaii.
5. <u>adjective</u>   Her room was <u>comfortable</u> and quiet.
6. <u>preposition</u> She liked to sit <u>on</u> her balcony.
7. <u>verb</u>   She <u>went</u> to the beach every day.
8. <u>noun</u>   She met many wonderful Hawaiian <u>people</u>.
9. <u>adjective</u>   Carla thinks Hawaiian culture is very <u>interesting</u>.
10. <u>adverb</u>   She's happy that she studied <u>hard</u> and wrote a great composition.

B
1. My friend Lin and I are in school from 8:00 to 12:00.
2. Our teacher is a kind man.
3. Our classes are interesting.
4. We learn a lot of English.
5. We sometimes have difficult homework.
6. We try to do our homework well.
7. Some students don't come to class every day.
8. Many students come to school every day.
9. Lin and I study hard every day.
10. Our class ends in June.

Review Test: Lessons 6–9

A
1. It is a very good job.
2. He was born in Russia 48 years ago.
3. They were/are very happy in Chile.
4. My father lives in China.
5. This is my brother.

B
1. Julia, Sophia, <u>and</u> Louise are all going to the store.
2. Should we go to the Thai restaurant <u>or</u> eat at the Indian restaurant?
3. I don't want to go hiking <u>because</u> I hurt my foot last week.
4. I really like Martin, <u>but</u> I don't like his sister at all!
5. Li has a lot of homework, <u>so</u> she's not going to the party.

C
1. Mylo <u>was</u> born in a small village.
2. He and his family <u>weren't</u> rich. They had a small farm.
3. When Mylo plays music at a concert, his wife and daughter <u>are</u> always with him.
4. His daughter <u>will be</u> two years old next week.
5. He <u>won't be</u> in Miami again soon.

REVIEW TESTS ANSWER KEY   **173**

D
1. After Charlie eats lunch, he takes a walk./Charlie takes a walk after he eats lunch.
2. Charlie takes a walk before he goes back to work./Before he goes back to work, Charlie takes a walk.
3. When Charlie gets home, he changes his clothes./Charlie changes his clothes when he gets home.
4. Charlie eats a snack before he has dinner./Before he has dinner, Charlie eats a snack.
5. After Charlie finishes reading, he goes to sleep./Charlie goes to sleep after he finishes reading.

Review Test: Lessons 10–13

A

1. Our neighbors (<u>make</u>/are making) a lot of noise every night. Their son (<u>plays</u>/is playing) the drums after dinner. He (plays/<u>is playing</u>) right now. I (think/<u>'m thinking</u>) about talking to his parents. My husband (<u>disagrees</u>/is disagreeing) with me. He (<u>thinks</u>/is thinking) the noise isn't a problem.

2. It's Saturday night, and Harry's restaurant (<u>is</u>/is being) almost empty! Usually, a lot of people (<u>come</u>/are coming) here on the weekends. But today, most people (listen/<u>are listening</u>) to music in the city park. Mylo (plays/<u>is playing</u>) a free concert right now. He often (<u>gives</u>/is giving) free concerts in the park.

B
1. I <u>didn't have</u> a good trip.
2. First, I almost <u>missed</u> my flight.
3. I <u>got</u> to Brazil late at night.
4. My girlfriend <u>didn't meet</u> me at the airport.
5. She <u>forgot</u> that I was coming to see her!
6. I <u>called</u> her on the phone.
7. She <u>wasn't</u> at home.
8. I <u>left</u> a message.
9. I <u>waited</u> two hours for her.
10. Finally, she <u>came</u> to get me. After that, the vacation was much better!

C
1. Many men used to have long hair when my father was young.
2. Did people used to think that the world was flat a long time ago?
3. One hundred years ago, the people in this town never used to travel during the winter.
4. People used to have a lot of children in the old days.
5. Did gas used to be 25 cents a gallon when you were young?
6. My father can remember when people didn't used to have televisions in their homes.
7. Did your sister used to travel much when she was young?
8. I remember when it used to cost two dollars to see a movie.
9. When I was a kid, many people never used to wear seat belts.
10. Did the milkman used to deliver bottles of milk to your parents' house?

Review Test: Lessons 14–17

A
1. Ivan: I'm going to go to a party. How about you?
   Tamon: I want to go to the library, but it's raining. I need a ride.
2. Ivan: Don't worry. I'll take you!
   Tamon: Thanks! I'm really worried about the test tomorrow.
3. Ivan: I'm sure that you'll pass the test.
4. Tamon: Mary is going to meet me at the library at 6:30. We have a 7:00 reservation at a restaurant for dinner.
5. Ivan: I hope that she won't be late.
   Tamon: She's always late!
6. Tamon: What are you going to do tomorrow?
7. Ivan: You don't remember? We planned it last week. You, Mary, Rebecca, and I are going to have a picnic in the park tomorrow afternoon.
8. Tamon: Oh, yeah! Hey, Mary hates cigarettes, so please don't smoke at the picnic.
   Ivan: Don't worry. I won't smoke.
9. Tamon: Thanks! Uh, we should buy some food for the picnic.
   Ivan: Yeah, you're right.
   Tamon: Will you come to the supermarket with me tomorrow? We can get it done early, like 8:00.
10. Ivan: No, I won't go that early. Tomorrow's Sunday. I want to sleep late. I'll go later.

B
1. Alice doesn't know what she (says/**will say**) if the interviewer (**asks**/will ask) about her job experience.
2. She (**is going to eat**/eats) something before she (**goes**/will go) to the interview.
3. After she (**eats**/will eat), Tom (**will help**/helps) her prepare for the interview.
4. Tom thinks that the interviewer (is/**will be**) impressed when he (**meets**/will meet) Alice.
5. When the interview (**is**/will be) finished, Alice (goes/**will go**) to the park.

C
1. On Thursday, Mary is visiting her parents.
2. On Friday, Mary is taking a math test.
3. On Sunday, Mary is flying to New York.
4. The flight leaves at 1 p.m.
5. The flight arrives at 5 p.m.

Review Test: Lessons 18–20

A
1. Were you born in China?
2. Do you like Australian schools?
3. Are you going to travel around Australia at the end of the year?
4. Did you make a lot of friends?
5. Are you studying hard for final exams?

B
1. When did he/Lee come to Australia?
2. How does he like our school?
3. Who is he living with now?
4. Why did he come here?
5. When will he return to China?

C

1. I asked him to <u>do</u> the dishes last night.
2. He <u>didn't</u> do them. The dirty dishes were still in the sink this morning.
3. Last week, I <u>did</u> all of the shopping.
4. Last night, I asked him, "<u>Did</u> you do the laundry?" He said, "No."
5. I am not going to <u>do</u> all of the chores anymore.

D

1. People in this house aren't doing their chores./People in this house don't do their chores.
2. Ricardo didn't clean the bathroom. Ricardo cleaned the bathroom.
3. When will Stephanie do the dishes?
4. Who washed the windows?
5. Makiko will do the shopping tomorrow.

Review Test: Lessons 21–24

A

1. Who is going to go to Poland?
2. How is she going/getting to Poland?
3. How long is the flight?
4. Who will she stay with in Warsaw?
5. Who else does she want to visit?
6. How far is her grandmother's house from her aunt and uncle's house?
7. How long does it take to drive there?
8. Who will she visit her grandmother with?
9. How often does Stan visit his grandmother?
10. How is his grandmother doing?

B

Anna: Tony, why <u>don't</u> we watch some TV?
Tony: Anna, it's 10:00. (1) <u>Doesn't</u> your class start at 10:00?
Anna: No, (2) <u>didn't</u> I tell you? I moved to the 11:00 class.
Tony: Oh, that's right. Well, we have an hour. Why (3) <u>don't</u> we go to the library? We can study.
Anna: (4) <u>Isn't</u> the library closed now?
Tony: No, it opens at 9:00.
Anna: But (5) <u>aren't</u> your parents coming this morning?
Tony: Oh, no! I forgot. They're probably at my apartment now!

C

1. No. I didn't grow up in Taipei.
2. No. I couldn't speak Chinese when I was a child.
3. No. I'm not happy living in New York City.
4. No. I'm not working at a very important company.
5. No. I'm not going to visit my family in Taiwan soon.

Review Test: Lessons 25–28

A

Martina: What a mess! Oh, look over there! (1. Who's/<u>Whose</u>) old bicycle is that?
Alberto: That's (2. <u>John's</u>/Johns'). The other bicycle over there is (3. my/<u>mine</u>).
Martina: (4. <u>It's</u>/Its) in really bad shape.
Alberto: Yes, it is.
Martina: And look over there. There's a stack of magazines. Are they Mary's?
Alberto: Yes, they're (5. her's/<u>hers</u>). She left them here when she went to college.

B

Sophie: Thanks. I have a report for him. He needs (1.) <u>it</u> fast.
Yukio: Well, he's actually busy right now. Some people from France came to talk to (2.) <u>him</u>.
Sophie: Is he meeting with (3.) <u>them</u> now?
Yukio: Yes. But maybe I can help (4.) <u>you</u>. I'm going into the meeting now. Just give (5.) <u>me</u> the report. I'll give it to Mr. Kim.
Sophie: Thanks!

C

I'm writing to you about Thanksgiving. I know that you and the kids want to come over for dinner. Honestly, I'm really worried about your kids. I'm sorry, but I have to talk to you about them. They help <u>themselves</u> to food and drinks without asking anyone. They also make a big mess. Ron and I have to clean it up. Last year, your son Harry fell down and hurt (1.) <u>himself</u>, and I was very upset. Ron and I can't enjoy (2.) <u>ourselves</u> when they're running around the house. Every year, I tell (3.) <u>myself</u> to just relax, but I can't. When you are at my house, I want you to make (4.) <u>yourself/yourselves</u> at home, but you still have to control your kids. You must tell them to behave (5.) <u>themselves</u>.

D

Linda: How did you like your birthday party?
Bob: I loved it, and I think that (<u>everybody</u>/anybody) had a good time.
Linda: Yes, I agree. (1. <u>No one</u>/Anyone) complained.
Bob: Hey, did you hear about Tom going to Hong Kong?
Linda: No, I haven't heard (2. something/<u>anything</u>) about it. Tell me (3. <u>everything</u>/anything) that you know!
Bob: I'd be happy to, but first let's talk about food. I'm going to get some Chinese food right now. Are you hungry? Do you want me to get you (4. <u>something</u>/nothing)?
Linda: Sure. I could eat (5. nothing/<u>anything</u>)!
Bob: Great! I'll be right back.

Review Test: Lessons 29–33

A

1. We'll need <u>a</u> flashlight, also.
2. Should we buy <u>Ø</u> sunscreen?
3. I think that we need <u>Ø</u> pillows.
4. I have <u>Ø</u> information about a good campground.
5. It may rain, so we should bring <u>an</u> umbrella.

B

1. There aren't (some/<u>any</u>) museums in my hometown.
2. There aren't many cars, so there is only (<u>a little</u>/a few) air pollution.
3. My town has (so many/<u>so much</u>) beautiful scenery.
4. I love my hometown, but I live in Los Angeles because I can make (<u>a lot of</u>/much) money here.
5. Sometimes I'm sad in Los Angeles because I have (any/<u>no</u>) friends here.

C

1. Today, I saw <u>the</u> same mice in the living room.
2. Except for mice, I really love <u>Ø</u> animals.
3. This morning, there was <u>a</u> big bird outside my window.
4. I think the big bird was <u>an</u> owl.
5. <u>The</u> owl flew off after about an hour.

D

1. I have three sisters. One lives in Rio de Janeiro. (The others/<u>The other</u>) sisters live in Paris.
2. My family keeps getting bigger. My oldest sister has three children. She just told me that she is going to have (<u>another</u>/the other one) baby.
3. I have three brothers. One of my brothers has two children. (<u>Another</u>/The other) has three children.
4. My oldest sister has four children. One is a girl. (The other/<u>The others</u>) are boys.
5. My youngest sister has two children. She wants to have (the others/<u>another one</u>).

E

1. I don't like computers because they are not reliable.
2. He went to the library to get a book.
3. Do they want another child/other children?
4. There is a lot of crime in my city!/There is too much crime in my city! It's dangerous here.
5. He gave me information about the statue and the bridge.

Review Test: Lessons 34–37

A

1. Maria is as old as Jorge.
2. Maria's sports car isn't as safe as Jorge's minivan.
3. Jorge drives as fast as Maria.
4. Jorge's vacation in Hawaii was not as expensive as Maria's vacation in Paris.
5. Hawaii was not as exciting as Paris.

B

1. Alberto lives near downtown. A man robbed him last week. He lost $75. Now he is afraid to go out at night. His neighborhood is (dangerous enough/<u>too dangerous</u>).
2. Yuriko lives in a big apartment. The rent is $2,000 a month. She makes $2,900 a month at her job. Her apartment is (expensive enough/<u>too expensive</u>).
3. Pierre and Helen have one child. They really want another child. They think that they (<u>don't have enough</u>/have too many) children.
4. Sally thinks people drive really fast near school. Herman agrees. He thinks that the people (don't drive fast enough/<u>drive too fast</u>).
5. Sam has a job at a factory. He earns $3,000 a month. He needs about $2,000 a month to pay his bills. Sam earns (<u>enough money</u>/too much money) to pay his bills.

C

1. Lee is funnier than Martin./Martin is less funny than Lee.
2. Swimming is better for your health than playing golf.
3. A sirloin steak is more expensive than a salad./A salad is less expensive than a sirloin steak.
4. Sasha's car is newer than Martina's car.
5. Tommy is friendlier than Marcus./Marcus is less friendly than Tommy.

D

1. Casper College has the most students.
2. Cogswell College has the best science department.
3. Jonesville College has the highest tuition.
4. Casper College has the cheapest dormitories.
5. Jonesville College has the largest library.

Review Test: Lessons 38–40

A
1. Many students <u>were reading</u> books.
2. After that, I went to the Student Union. A lot of people <u>were playing</u> cards.
3. When I left, everyone <u>was talking</u> loudly.
4. The sun <u>was shining</u> and it was really warm.
5. A group of my friends <u>were swimming</u> in the pool.

B
1. police officer: <u>What was the maid doing</u> at that time?
   John: The maid was cleaning the library.
2. police officer: <u>Who was talking</u> with her?
   John: Harry was talking with her.
3. police officer: <u>Why was Harry talking</u> to the maid?
   John: I don't know why Harry was talking with her.
4. police officer: <u>Was Martin talking</u> with her then?
   John: No, Martin wasn't talking with her then. He was in the kitchen at that time.
5. police officer: <u>When was Martin talking</u> with her?
   John: Martin was talking with her later, around 9:00.

C
1. People (ⓒame/were coming) from all over the world.
2. The artist's plane (ⓐrrived/was arriving) late.
3. At 9:00, everyone (still waited/ⓦas still waiting) for her.
4. While the artist (riding/ⓦas riding) in the taxi from the airport, the people were eating. Then they started to go home.
5. When the artist finally (ⓖot/was getting) there, the food and the people were gone.

D
1. Why was Chen studying for a test last night?
2. Were the children doing their homework when their father came home?
3. At 7:30 in the morning, everyone was still sleeping.
4. While Mary was driving, Andrew was looking out the window./Andrew was looking out the window while Mary was driving.
5. While Mr. Jang was cooking dinner, the children watched TV./Mr. Jang was cooking dinner while the children watched TV.

Review Test: Lessons 41–45

A
   Marianne is a student at a community college in New Jersey. She is living in a small town in central New Jersey. <u>Living</u> in New Jersey is very exciting for her. She can go to New York City on the weekends, and she enjoys <u>being</u> near farms and fields during the week. She likes her town because her neighbors are nice, and there isn't much crime or pollution. She dislikes <u>taking</u> the long bus ride to school every day, but her classes are all interesting. <u>Studying</u> computer programs is difficult for Marianne, but she likes <u>trying</u> to understand difficult things. She is having problems <u>learning</u> English right now, but she has a good time <u>talking</u> with students from many different countries in her English class. Her best friend Olivia is from the Czech Republic and is studying math. Marianne was thinking about <u>staying</u> in the United States after graduation, but <u>returning</u> to her country seems like a better idea now. She is having a hard time <u>being</u> away from her family so much. She likes <u>going</u> home during vacations, but it's not enough.

B
1. There was some (<u>exciting</u>/excited) music, but nobody danced.
2. The people talked about (<u>boring</u>/bored) subjects, like football.
3. The discussions about politics weren't (<u>interesting</u>/interested).
4. Most people seemed (relaxing/<u>relaxed</u>).
5. They may just have been (tiring/<u>tired</u>).
6. The best part of the party was the food. Martina brought an (<u>amazing</u>/amazed) garlic soup.
7. Mark told a (<u>frightening</u>/frightened) story about a burglary in the neighborhood.
8. Henry was (embarrassing/<u>embarrassed</u>) because he dropped a big bowl of potato chips on the carpet.
9. The hostess wasn't (annoying/<u>annoyed</u>), however. She just vacuumed up the chips.
10. There were a lot of nice people at the party, but I was still (disappointing/<u>disappointed</u>).

C
1. The class is very <u>interesting</u>.
2. The teacher makes the class very active, so I'm never <u>bored</u>.
3. Last semester, I <u>was working</u> as an intern in an elementary school.
4. I <u>am graduating</u> this semester, so I'll start looking for a teaching job very soon.
5. <u>Working</u> as a teacher will be a fantastic career.

Review Test: Lessons 46–49

A
Dear Ms. Johnston,
   Thank you for your nice letter. Yes, your son John arrived safely. He is happy <u>to be</u> here in Los Angeles. He has a very active life. He likes <u>to hike</u> in the Rocky Mountains. He started <u>to take</u> classes in scuba diving last month. He wants <u>to go</u> to San Diego in December <u>to dive</u>. He enjoys most sports. I will tell him <u>to write</u> you a long letter this weekend.

B
1. He went to Canada (<u>to attend</u>/attending) a good university.
2. Now, he's having a hard time (to study/<u>studying</u>).
3. He enjoys (to have/<u>having</u>) fun at night with friends.
4. He avoids (to attend/<u>attending</u>) classes that he doesn't like.
5. He doesn't like (to do/<u>doing</u>) his homework.
6. My wife and I are very worried that he will start (to get/<u>getting</u>) bad grades.
7. We want him (<u>to succeed</u>/succeeding) in his studies.
8. He plans (<u>to go</u>/going) to medical school after he gets his degree.
9. He will have to start (to work/<u>working</u>) much harder.
10. You have to be a good student (<u>to get</u>/getting) into medical school.

C
1. She often needs to hire new employees.
2. She enjoys working with people.
3. It is sometimes difficult to work such long hours.
4. She often works on weekends to get more business.
5. My mother is able to increase the number of her customers.
6. Correct.
7. She planned to visit me at my university.
8. She would like to see me again.
9. I am considering going home for Christmas.
10. I can't wait to see her again.

Review Test: Lessons 50–53

A
1. The teacher handed **it** out.
2. We all looked **them** over.
3. I had to put **it** off because of my job.
4. The teachers let us make **it** up.
5. The teacher called on **him** five times.

B
1. My boss used to look my figures <u>over</u> closely every day at 5:00.
2. She found <u>out</u> that I was doing a really good job.
3. I succeeded <u>in</u> earning her trust.
4. Now she is talking <u>about</u> promoting me to a better job.
5. I look forward <u>to</u> having more responsibility and a better salary.
6. She thinks that I am capable <u>of</u> being a store manager someday.
7. She knows that I get along <u>with</u> my co-workers.
8. I ran <u>into</u> my old friend John last week.
9. He wasn't surprised <u>by</u> my success.

C
1. She is tired of working for a low salary.
2. She is now responsible for training new employees.
3. Correct.
4. New employees need information, and Imelda looks it up for them.
5. Imelda is good at her job, but she is bored.
6. In the past, Imelda was afraid of looking for a new job.
7. She believes in working hard to succeed in life.
8. She is interested in getting a more challenging job.
9. She just got a new job at a company that is famous for making computers.
10. Imelda will certainly succeed in/at reaching her goals.

Review Test: Lessons 54–58

A

Brad: Are you ready for the camping trip?
Brandi: Almost. I have everything on the bed, but I still <u>have to</u> put it in my backpack.
Brad: Did you bring warm clothes? It (1.) <u>might/could/may</u> be cold tonight. We'll be in the mountains.
Brandi: Yes, I did. Are you ready?
Brad: I'm packed, but now I have a headache.
Brandi: You (2.) <u>should</u> take an aspirin. It always helps me.
Brad: You're right. Hey, where's Harry? He's late.
Brandi: Yeah, he left his house an hour ago. There (3.) <u>must/could/may/might be</u> a lot of traffic.
Brad: Well, I hope he gets here soon. I want to leave on time.
Brandi: You (4.) <u>shouldn't/don't have to</u> worry so much. We'll be just fine.
Brad: OK. I'll relax. Hey, don't let me forget. We have almost no gas in the van. We (5.) <u>have to</u> stop at a gas station.
Brandi: OK. Oh, look. Harry just got here!

B

1. Where should we buy it?
2. Do we have to pay cash?
3. Do we have to buy it today?
4. When should we give the bike to Tommy?/When should we give Tommy the bike?
5. Should we drive to the store in my car?

C

Martin: I'm doing fine, Brandi. Did you and your friends (1.) <u>go</u> camping?
Brandi: Yeah. But we had to (2.) <u>find</u> a new campground. Pinewoods Park is closed now.
Martin: That's too bad. We used to (3.) <u>have</u> a lot of fun there.
Brandi: I really enjoyed (4.) <u>hiking</u> there. But Harp's Meadow is open. Let's go there today.
Martin: I'd like to go there today, but I <u>am helping</u> my mom clean the house right now.

D

1. It used to be a really nice house.
2. We had to do a lot of repair work.
3. My husband didn't take care of himself.
4. Correct.
5. He hurt himself and may be in the hospital for a week.

Review Test: Lessons 59–61

A

1. eaten   2. gone   3. learned   4. been   5. had

B

1. She has been married.
2. She has gone skiing./She has been skiing.
3. She has worked for Federal Accounting for one year.
4. She has visited Paris./She has been to Paris.
5. She/Joy has lived in the house for two years.

C
1. They have been close friends <u>since</u> last year.
2. Abe has lived in Hawaii <u>since</u> December.
3. Abe has worked as a carpenter <u>for</u> ten years.
4. Joy has been an accountant <u>since</u> she graduated from college.
5. Abe has been sick <u>for</u> two days.

D
1. Has Abe ever taught sports?
2. Have Abe and Joy ever gone/been to China?
3. Have they ever scuba dived/gone scuba diving/been scuba diving?
4. Has Joy ever gone hiking/been hiking/hiked?
5. Have they ever eaten Japanese food?

E
1. Has Eleanor's father ever visited you?
2. Yes, he has come to our house two times.
3. We have rarely seen my parents since we moved here.
4. Correct.
5. I have gone/been back to my country only twice.

Review Test: Lessons 62–64

A
Todd: Yes, I've (1.) <u>already</u> done my homework. But I haven't done my chores (2.) yet.
Mother: Why haven't you done your chores (3.) <u>yet</u>?
Todd: I haven't had time. Has Mary come back from the store (4.) <u>yet</u>?
Mother: Yes, she's (5.) <u>already</u> gotten back. She came back an hour ago.

B
Martha: John, (1. how many times/<u>how long</u>) have you lived here?
John: I've lived here for three years.
Martha: What do you do?
John: I'm a flight attendant. I work on jets flying to Europe.
Martha: Really? (2. <u>How many times</u>/How long) have you flown to Paris?
John: I've gone to Paris more times than I can count! I just got back from Paris yesterday.
Martha: That's incredible! I've only been to Paris (3. <u>twice</u>/ever).
John: It *is* really nice to go to Europe so often, but I'm actually very tired of my job.
Martha: (4. How many times/<u>How long</u>) have you been a flight attendant?
John: (5. <u>Since I moved here.</u>/Since three years.) What do you do, Martha?
Martha: I'm a criminal lawyer. I just graduated from law school last year.
John: That must be exciting! (6. <u>How many times</u>/How long) have you gone to court?
Martha: I've gone to court ten times. It's interesting, but it's stressful!

C

Raoul: It was great! I (1.) <u>saw</u> all of my relatives in Nicaragua.
Kim: I'd love to go there. I (2.) <u>haven't ever been/'ve never been</u> to Central America.
Raoul: You should go. You (3.) <u>studied</u> Spanish last semester, right?
Kim: Yes. I (4.) <u>have taken</u> three Spanish classes since I started studying at this school.
Raoul: Wow, that's great. Where (5.) <u>did</u> you <u>go</u> for your vacation?
Kim: I didn't go anywhere. I stayed here in Indianapolis. My aunt and uncle visited me.

D

1. Why haven't you finished the report (yet)?/Why haven't you finished it (yet)?
2. How long have you needed that expense information?
3. Have you asked him for the information (yet)?
4. Did he give you some information yesterday?/Didn't he give you some information yesterday?
5. How many times has he been late with important information?